Amazing GRACE

Donald P. Mangum
Brenton G. Yorgason

BOOKCRAFT
Salt Lake City, Utah

Library of Congress Catalog Card Number: 96-84787
ISBN 1-57008-239-1

First Printing, 1996

Printed in the United States of America

For Mitch

God's Way

God's chief way of acting is by persuasion and patience and long-suffering, not by coercion and stark confrontation. He acts by gentle solicitation and by sweet enticement. He always acts with unfailing respect for the freedom and independence that we possess. He wants to help us and pleads for the chance to assist us, but he will not do so in violation of our agency. . . .

To countermand and ultimately forbid our choices was Satan's way, not God's, and the Father of us all simply never will do that. He will, however, stand by us forever to help us see the right path, find the right choice, respond to the true voice, and feel the influence of his undeniable Spirit. His gentle, peaceful, powerful persuasion to do right and find joy will be with us "so long as time shall last, or the earth shall stand, or there shall be one man upon the face thereof to be saved" (Moroni 7:36).

—Howard W. Hunter

Contents

Acknowledgments

We thank our dear friends and loved ones who have lived this writing dream with us, and who have offered insights and encouragement at crucial moments along the way. Of these, we especially thank Robert and Helen Wells, Ron and Jan Johnson, Larry and Londa Jeppesen, Bill and Betty Thurston, Dave Tolman, Dan Bell, Dee Darling, John and Maryanne Zeller, Phil Lear, Bill Bush, Steve and Liz Swanson, Larry and Marie Gunther, Rod Davies, Lorin Nielsen, Bob Chatfield, and Denney Pugmire.

We have likewise appreciated the profound insights offered and assistance rendered by our companions, Diane and Margaret. This book is much better written because of their input.

The Mangum family would like to give special heartfelt thanks to the members, former and current, of the Hingham Ward and Hingham Stake in southeastern Massachusetts. From these dear souls they have learned much about grace—kindness and love given to them at the time of their son Mitch's passing. They feel undeserving of the proffered generous and thoughtful caring, but have gratefully accepted it.

Finally, we thank our eight missionary sons—missionaries both past and present—who continue to teach us the spiritual nuggets of their own learning. These are, in order of service, Donald, Marc, Jason, Aaron, Jeremy, Mitch, Josh, and Adam. We credit their mothers for rearing them even as Helaman's warriors were reared—in obedience and humility before the Lord. We're hopeful that their younger brothers—Don, Matt, Dave, Sam, and Jordan—will also choose to serve the Lord full time when they reach the age of nineteen. Our three daughters, Rachel, Jennifer, and Angela, are likewise jewels of righteousness and hopefully future full-time missionaries, and for their influence and discerning spirits we will forever be grateful.

Prologue

Although we now find it hard to believe, our relationship extends over thirty-five years. We attended rival high schools in Provo, Utah—Don at Provo High and Brent at Brigham Young High. We were a year apart in school, with Don being eleven months Brent's senior, but had many common friends. In our uncomplicated adolescent minds we viewed each other with some suspicion, while outwardly being gracious toward each other.

We met again a decade later, in Salt Lake City; this time as returned missionaries, college graduates, and fellow laborers in the Church Educational System. We both were teaching seminary—Brent at East High School and Don at South High.

Rekindling our high school memories, we soon became good friends. Three years later we both left CES and traveled back to Provo to pursue graduate studies at Brigham Young University. During this time, we also became business partners.

As the years passed, Brent's family moved to Sandy, Utah, where Don lived, and we enjoyed being neighbors. Without question, gospel service together strengthened our friendship. Don's family eventually moved to New England, and professionally we went our separate ways. Even so, our friendship has deepened to this day.

The decision to coauthor this book was not an easy one. Because of the sacred nature of the topic, we felt an obligation to proceed cautiously and carefully. While deeply respectful of each other's understanding of the Atonement, we wanted to "come together" and reflect a mutual understanding and perspective. This, in fact, has happened.

Don offers these thoughts about how this book evolved across those many miles between Utah and Massachusetts: My friendship with Brent has lasted many years. During the course of our meandering through life together, we have often talked about gospel principles and how they apply in our lives. We had a wonderful experience serving together in a stake presidency; and then, when my family and I moved to New England, we continued to stay in touch. We have spent what seems to be hundreds of wonderful hours sharing ideas and experiences by telephone. About five years later, we began talking about the tender mercies of the Lord. We talked about his grace and the Atonement in more depth than we ever had before. As those conversations deepened, Brent's almost automatic reaction—based upon years of writing experience—was that we should write a book about these concepts. To me, the thought of coauthoring a book was foreign but one that I have gradually accepted. Perhaps, I considered, there are some thoughts here that would help others more fully understand the concept of grace. Our simple goal is to encourage those who read these pages to not give up in life, to keep at it, and to have true hope in the atonement of Christ—which hope makes all necessary things possible.

Brent adds: Those who know Don appreciate the fact that his mind is uncommonly quick. I didn't know this when he and I first met as teenagers, but I have come not only to admire his mental abilities but to cling to them as I stretch out along my own learning curve. While Don and I have walked much of life's path together, it was not until three years ago that we began to truly internalize the meaning of the Savior's atonement. Our learning pace accelerated until at last we found ourselves crystallizing thoughts and sequences like never before. Truly, my journey of discovery with Don has been—and continues to be—one of my life's treasures.

As authors and lay teachers of the gospel, our perspectives and our capacities are finite. On the other hand, the principle of grace is infinite and eternal. Thus, any finite person trying to explore and explain such a principle will fall short. It is likely that few of us in our lifetimes will fully comprehend the atonement of Christ or the attendant principle of grace. In a real way, therefore, it feels presumptuous for the two of us to submit for publication an incomplete, unfinished discussion. However, knowing the joy that has come from *our* growing appreciation of the Savior's grace, we hope that the materials contained herein will likewise add to *your* joy and fulfillment.

This book is intended to be a "no guilt" reading experience. In the context of this book, the idea of "no guilt" is used to encourage us to not feel forced to measure up or to go out and do unusual things that individuals in this book may have done. Each of us has unique talents, abilities, gifts, and limitations—as well as our own divinely crafted ladders of progression. Thus, we will be held accountable to simply measure up to our heavenly designed yardstick.

We believe that understanding and implementing the saving principle of grace must be done individually. That is, all must gain a personal testimony of the power of Christ's atonement, and then make this testimony operational as they move up the ladder toward exaltation. However, though we must climb onto the first rung of this ladder alone, we would do well to position it alongside the ladders of our friends and loved ones and to join hands as we climb together. This will then allow us to progress in our own way, while giving and receiving personalized assistance and encouragement.

As authors—both in our personal lives as well as throughout the nearly four decades of our association with each other—we have always felt safety in following the teachings of the Brethren, both ancient and modern. In writing this book, it has been our guiding philosophy to always try to have our thoughts and impressions reflect this loyalty and commitment. Nevertheless, we are solely responsible for the information and conclusions contained herein.

The pages that follow are the results of an unfinished journey of discovery. We have sought to avoid a preachy presentation of gospel doctrine. Rather, we have desired to share some ideas that have changed our lives or the lives of others. To facilitate the presentation of our impressions, we use a variety of methods: Sometimes we simply share directly our thoughts and ideas. In other cases we create fictional groups and settings in which people discuss relevant topics. We also use several real events as they were related directly to us. With the exception of people mentioned in our own personal experiences and Elder Robert E. Well's story, the characters in this book are fictional. Even so, the experiences shared are true, regardless of the manner of presentation. These varied approaches thus become the means by which we speak and teach of Christ's atoning sacrifice. We hope you enjoy these styles of sharing true and sometimes poignant moments, just as we have enjoyed putting them to pen.

Additionally, we have attempted to be true to the evolution of our understanding of grace as it has unfolded and continues to unfold for us. Don is typically an anecdotal learner. That is, he looks for meanings in parables and in the life stories of others as well as in his own experiences. When he discovered concepts related to grace that were new to him—both in anecdotes and by experience—he shared them with Brent. Once shared, he and Brent would bounce these ideas back and forth until they became clearer to both of them. These ideas were recorded in this book, with Brent adding experiences and impressions of his own.

In chapter 1, Don describes the origin of his focus on the central theme of grace. Once this concept had begun to take shape in his mind, he shared it with Brent, and from there the following evolution of mutually shared ideas took place.

Finally, the experience shared by Elder Robert E. Wells is true and is as he recorded it for his family history. We deeply appreciate his trust in allowing us to share his personal and sacred reflection in this public setting.

As you begin reading the pages that follow, perhaps it would be well to remember the words of the prophet Nephi: "I, Nephi, will show unto you that *the tender mercies of the Lord* are over all those whom he hath chosen, because of their faith, to make them mighty even unto the power of deliverance" (1 Nephi 1:20; emphasis added).

PART 1

A Change of Mind:
Making a
Case for Grace

On 9 April 1945 at a concentration camp in Flossenburg, Germany, a young Lutheran minister, Dietrich Bonhoeffer, was hanged by the neck until he was dead. This brutal and unnecessary execution was conducted by S.S. Black Guards under special order from Heinrich Himmler, one of Hitler's chief henchmen. Ironically, though somehow not surprisingly, this murder of a thirty-nine-year-old Christian leader occurred just a few days before the camp was liberated by the Allies.

Bonhoeffer was a remarkable Christian theologian whose life deserves a place of honor in the annals of Christianity. He was fearless when confronted directly by the grotesque evil of Nazism, wickedness at an intensity that is difficult for the rational mind to comprehend. Because he had been an outspoken critic of the godless tyranny that seized Germany by the throat and that threatened to strangle the life out of a country rich in culture and history, Bonhoeffer was in peril almost from the moment that Hitler began his frightening ascension to power.

At an early age, Bonhoeffer gained respect among prominent Christians in his homeland as an outspoken critic of the Third Reich. When the evil forces began to gain control in Germany, Bonhoeffer spoke out boldly against them. His friends in the Lutheran Church sought to save his life. In doing so, they sneaked him out of the country.

His escape took him to the United States, and then for a time to England; but he soon returned to Germany. He could not, in good conscience, remain elsewhere. In spite of the pleading of his friends, Bonhoeffer increased his overt objections to the sinister activities that pervaded his beloved country.

To his friends, who had encouraged him to stay in the relative comfort of Great Britain, he simply indicated that to linger in safety would be unconscionable. How could he hide when his parishioners were in peril? If he waited until it was safe to return, what would he tell those who had suffered through the conflict? With a determined resolve, he went home to face evil incarnate. Fearless and filled with conviction, he stared, without blinking, into the eyes of his adversaries. So they imprisoned him.

With the courage known to Joseph of Egypt, to Saul of Damascus, and to Joseph of Liberty, he also ministered to those around him during his incarceration. Finding himself behind physical barriers, he gave spiritual comfort. The guards who held him captive were so moved by his demeanor—and by his acts of charity and compassion among the other prisoners—that they smuggled his writings out of the dungeon. These writings were then given to his friends, who later had them published in book form.

His thoughts, many of which were written while in prison, were translated into English, some of which are in a book titled *The Cost of Discipleship*.[1] This book should be read by all those who love liberty, freedom, and Christianity. Bonhoeffer was truly a martyr for the cause of Christ. For that alone he deserves to be remembered, honored, and revered.

However, it is not because of his martyrdom that Bonhoeffer is included in the introductory chapter of this book. In fact, it was not his death that caused us to notice him. Rather, it was his marvelously insightful statements about the Atonement that made him stand out. He wrote about his relationship with Christ in a precise, insightful, and unforgettable way.

"When Christ calls a man," he wrote, "he bids him come and die."[2] Regardless of the identity of the author, these provocative words create a rich image of true Christian response. This powerful sentence, however, creates some confusion when we realize that it was written by a Lutheran minister. Let us remember that it was Martin Luther who laid the groundwork for the doctrine of salvation by *profession* of faith only—not by the energy and commitment expended by the individual Christian. That doctrine, attributed to Luther, has been called "salvation by grace." This religious concept was taught by many of Bonhoeffer's peers and remains a central belief in many present-day Christian sects, including modern-day Lutheranism.

Nonetheless, the young minister of Hitler's Germany taught a doctrine quite different from that of his peers. His active rejection of what he called "cheap grace" was more significant than his opposition to the Third Reich. While Nazism created jeopardy for the body, the doctrine of salvation by grace, and grace alone, created peril for the soul. So taught Bonhoeffer, and so it is.

Bonhoeffer's sermons, from pulpits in his native land as well as on foreign soil, were filled with a spirit of grateful appreciation for the almost unfathomable magnitude of grace demonstrated by the Master. In his writings he described the deep commitment that should accompany the acceptance of Christ's grace. His description of the requirements made upon people by Christianity may be unparalleled in any modern Christian teacher's writings outside of The Church of Jesus Christ of Latter-day Saints.

The final irony concerning Bonhoeffer, in our present discussion, is that prior to writing this book, as we studied both the doctrine of grace and the writings of Bonhoeffer, we found ourselves across the spectrum from him. On one end of that continuum is the concept of cheap grace; that is, "the preaching of forgiveness without requiring repentance."[3] In the center is the concept shared by Bonhoeffer of costly grace, meaning that "grace is costly because it compels a man to submit to the yoke of Christ and follow him."[4] Still further to the right of this spectrum is where we found ourselves. We didn't believe in cheap grace, nor did we simply believe in costly grace, as Bonhoeffer defined it. We believed salvation was so costly that normal people could not attain it. Thus, if we truly believed in grace at all, it was in a grace *so costly* that it made salvation almost impossible.

As students of the gospel, we have sought the true doctrine of grace. This book is a discussion about our attempts to

find it. The correct doctrine is truly found in The Church of
Jesus Christ of Latter-day Saints. We had just been too busy
to uncover it. As you will see, the continuing process of discovering true grace is the subject of this book.

————NOTES

1. See Dietrich Bonhoeffer, *The Cost of Discipleship* (New York:
Macmillan Publishing Co., 1963).
2. Ibid., p. 99.
3. Ibid., p. 47.
4. Ibid., p. 48.

CHAPTER ONE

The Keystone—
Pathway to the Cornerstone

> I told the brethren that the Book of Mormon was the most correct of any book on earth, and the *keystone* of our religion, and a man would get nearer to God by abiding by its precepts, than by any other book.
>
> —Joseph Smith

> [Ye are] of the household of God; and are built upon the foundation of the apostles and prophets, Jesus Christ himself being the chief corner stone.
>
> —Ephesians 2:19–20

Brent and I (Don) have often reflected on a well-known story called "The Three Princes of Serendip." This story describes desirable discoveries made by accident, from which the word *serendipity* evolved. The use of this word is convenient when one makes such a discovery and cannot tell for sure how such a moment came about. When real treasures are uncovered amidst the common, everyday activities of life, it just seems too good to be true, but it isn't.

During the late fall of 1989, I was sitting in a typical high council meeting. If you haven't been to one, I don't necessarily recommend it for treasure hunting—there is just nothing particularly unique about a high council meeting. However, at the end of the meeting one of the high councilors was invited to bear his testimony.

In his testimony my friend told us that he had read the Book of Mormon every year since President Ezra Taft Benson had challenged Church members to study it daily. This seemingly ordinary expression of conviction changed my life. You see, I'm embarrassed to say that I hadn't completed the Book of Mormon even once since being admonished by our then-living prophet to read it. Clearly, I had ignored the counsel from the prophet for several years. While listening to this simple testimony, something stirred within me. That very night I decided to finish the Book of Mormon by the end of that year. It wasn't one of those deep resolves a person makes and for which he'll move heaven and earth. It was just a regular old commitment, like those I had made countless times in the past. Maybe it would really happen, and maybe it wouldn't.

As the meeting drew to a close, I opened my copy of the Book of Mormon and confirmed that it contained 531 pages. It was early November, and there were a little more than fifty days left in the year. By doing a little easy math, I determined that if I read ten pages a day, I would finish by year end, with a few days left over for good behavior. It seemed simple enough to me. That night I made a fairly firm commitment to get started—tomorrow—and I drove home feeling pretty good about myself.

When I awoke the next day, however, my resolve had almost disappeared—like the morning dew before the rising sun. Remnants of the commitment remained, though, and after a week or two I sat down to review my progress. There were then about thirty days left in the year and I had read a few pages, so I was left with seventeen pages to read per day to complete the task by the end of the year. Having finished the calculation, I promised myself I would really get rolling—tomorrow.

As you might guess, I continued to be better at math than with my follow-through. Thus, during the next two weeks I read a little, but not nearly enough. When there were two weeks left in the year, I still had about 450 pages to go. The calculation was still simple, but the task now seemed a lot more imposing. But, I thought, maybe I could really get going between Christmas and the New Year.

At year's end, I found that I had done better with this reading goal than with some similar projects in the past. In fact, I had completed almost half of the Book of Mormon. Not great, but really not bad. I was encouraged.

On January first, between football games, I went into my study to consider my reading project. I noted that I had read about three hundred pages. Being left-brained, I really enjoy mathematical relationships, so I was intrigued with the thought of reading ten pages a day. The number ten is even, it divides easily into everything, and if I read that much each day I would finish by the end of January—very tidy and very appealing to my left-brained tendencies.

This time, however, I really meant it! I started reading ten pages every day. After a few days at this pace, which surprisingly I sustained, I advanced into much less familiar territory. Two or three weeks passed, and to my amazement I had kept at it.

On January 31 I completed the last page of the book, then closed it with a modest sense of satisfaction. I felt those familiar, warm sensations of the Spirit confirming that what I had read really did come from above. If that was all that came from this first effort, it would have been sufficient.

For a moment I considered my goal to complete the Book of Mormon. Because my reading project had straddled two years, I wondered if I would get credit for reading it both years, 1989 and 1990. An interesting question, but I wasn't sure whom to ask, nor was I sure if anyone was keeping track of such things.

More important, on that day I crystallized something that I had been thinking about as I was completing my first reading of the Book of Mormon. Remembering my fellow high councilor's testimony, I concluded that reading ten pages a day wasn't really all that difficult, and it had been quite spiritually uplifting. I decided to start reading the Book of Mormon again at the same pace.

After sixty more days, or about the end of March, I finished again. This time the reading had taken on a slightly different character. In the past, whenever I had read the first few pages of the book, the story was so familiar I could almost quote it. I think I know this part of Nephi's story better than he does. While he "only" experienced it, it seems that I have read it two or three times a year since the Book of Mormon was translated.

This time, undaunted by the familiarity of Nephi's story, I simply pressed forward. But when I came to some of the chapters in Mosiah and Alma, *they* were familiar—not as familiar as 1 Nephi, but still I could anticipate the content of coming verses in a way that I hadn't ever done before. Such anticipation gave a richer understanding of what the prophets were saying and the nature of the events as they occurred in the stories.

On the first of April I started reading the Book of Mormon again at about the same pace. I stopped thinking about any resolve or commitment, other than to keep pressing doggedly forward. As I came to passages I had read within the past two months, my familiarity with these pages added a flavor to the content that I had never before experienced.

By the end of May, two things happened: One, I had finished the Book of Mormon for the third time. More important, the repetitive coursing through the passages written by inspired prophets was leading me to important and life-altering discoveries.

Let me explain: Almost every day I was spending about thirty minutes reading the Book of Mormon . . . day after day after day. While at first I thought I was just reading familiar stories about the Nephites and their history, it was much more than that. You see, I didn't know then that 50 percent of the verses in the Book of Mormon mention Christ. So every day I was spending much of my thirty minutes of reading time immersed in discussions of Christ by prophets.

I also was unaware at the time that while the word *atonement* appears in the New Testament only once, the Book of Mormon uses the word twenty-eight times. Further, the Book of Mormon prophets wrote almost countless passages addressing the meaning and power of the Atonement in our lives. So with some regularity I was being exposed to profound discussions about the nature and effects of the Atonement. Further, there were wonderful and comforting discussions about grace within the pages of the Nephite record.

Now, in May, when I completed the third reading, I didn't know these details about how the Savior and his mission are portrayed in the Book of Mormon. But I did know that this intense reading project had taken on a life and direction of its own.

Sometime during the spring or early summer of that year, I determined that I could keep up this pace for the balance of the year. Wanting to have a focused reading experience, I began to search for a topic. At first I considered emphasizing the sometimes confusing Book of Mormon geography. I even bought several books by LDS archaeologists to help with the study. However, as someone reminded me, the Book of Mormon is not a second witness for geography. So I abandoned geography and looked for another topic. I had often heard it said that we don't really understand Christ's sacrifice—neither in Gethsemane nor on the cross. In the past, when I heard comments like this I believed that they applied to me, but I wasn't sure how to change my understanding. Thinking of these things, I made a simple resolve to focus my future reading on the Atonement.

So, sometime about midyear, again somewhat matter-of-factly, I purchased a new hardbound missionary version of the Book of Mormon. I then began marking all the passages that pertained to Christ, the Atonement, the concept of grace, and other related doctrines.

If that had been the end of it, I would have considered myself richly blessed. It wasn't the end, however, but only the beginning. By December 31, in continuing my reading pace I had completed the book about seven times within a twelve-month period. I had also continued marking passages about the mission of Christ. Through this project I learned more about his life and his love for us than I had previously understood.

Looking back upon the reading experience of that year, I found myself identifying with the citizens of the fictitious city of Serendip. Because of a simple testimony in a high council meeting during the early days of a cold New England winter, I had discovered valuable treasures, seemingly by accident.

The Apostle Paul referred to Christ as the cornerstone of the Church. The Prophet Joseph identified the Book of Mormon as the keystone of our religion. This keystone is preeminent in the archway which opens the path that leads to the Church of Christ and to a more complete understanding of the Cornerstone. The path to the Cornerstone is strait and narrow, and filled with treasures beyond our expectations!

Authors' note: After Don's twelve-month reading experience, Brent said, "If Don can do that, so can anyone!" Thus, on 1 January 1991 Brent began reading the Book of Mormon at a rate of ten pages each day. By the end of that year he had also finished the Book of Mormon seven times. These experiences helped set the stage for what follows in this book.

CHAPTER TWO

A Gospel of Works,
a Gospel of Grace

During our somewhat intense experience reading the Book of Mormon and studying the doctrine of the Atonement, we began to reflect more and more upon the implications of what we read. We came to the realization that there were fundamental doctrines related to the Atonement that we had previously failed to understand. We felt that we were in the group described by Elder Bruce R. McConkie in his final general conference address: "Many of us have a superficial knowledge [of the Atonement] and rely upon the Lord and his goodness to see us through the trials and perils of life."[1]

Without realizing it at first, our studies were changing our understanding of the Atonement, the preeminent doctrine of the Savior's gospel. As we continued to study the mission of Christ, we discovered ideas about the doctrine of grace that were new to us, though clearly taught by the ancient and modern prophets. Because we had never given this kind of attention to the meaning and application of grace, our understanding had been incomplete.

In order to facilitate a presentation of some of the newly discovered ideas, we thought it might be helpful to imagine a fictional but typical Gospel Doctrine Sunday School class.

We, the authors, and you, the readers, will be silent and un-seen guests in the classroom. We can hear and see everything going on in the room, but they cannot see or hear us.

Brother Randy Thomas is the Gospel Doctrine teacher. He is an instructor at a local university, well respected by ward members and truly seasoned in gospel scholarship. He appropriately views himself as a facilitator, trying to encourage class members to read assigned scriptures each week, then come to class ready for discussion. This year the course of study is the Book of Mormon, and on this particular day the subject of grace comes up. Brother Thomas asks these questions of the class: "What do you think *grace* means as it is used in the scriptures?" And "How does grace apply to the gospel generally and to your life in particular?" For the next forty-five minutes a lively discussion ensues.

Brother Tom Wilson, always ready with an answer, raises his hand and begins his response by saying, "I have long believed that the Savior's atonement is similar to gravity. It is always there, in place for everyone. If I just sit, gravity holds me to the Earth. This is like the resurrection; it is there for everyone. We can just sit there and do nothing, and we will be resurrected. However, if I want to take advantage of the benefits of the Atonement or of gravity, I have to *act*. His grace puts both gravity and the Atonement in place. However, as a practical matter, I think that in this life it all really depends on me, simply because the Atonement is already in place for any and all who qualify. If I fail to act, I simply fail. Thus, my understanding of grace is this: by his grace the Atonement was put in place, but it is up to me—solely by myself—to take advantage of it."

As we look around the room, several heads nod in affirmation. Then, adding to this notion, Sister Becky Strong raises her hand and speaks. "Brother Thomas, you know that I am really into running. So maybe a metaphor about running will be useful." Becky has just returned from Boston, where she completed the Boston Marathon.

She continues, "I think I see the tasks related to exaltation as a marathon, where I am the runner. In the marathon, when the gun goes off and the race begins, everything is up to each individual participant. In my view of salvation, which term is synonymous with exaltation in the scriptures, I believe that it is really up to me. Grace comes into play if I come close to the finish line—very close—then Christ will come out and pull me across; but I had better get close enough! Again, his coming out to help me across the line is grace; but the largest part—say about 26.1 miles of the 26.2 miles of it—is up to me."

Again, several heads nod in agreement, and there is some murmuring of acknowledgment as well. Almost immediately Richard Jackson, our resident certified public accountant, raises his hand.

"As long as we're going the analogy route," he begins, "let me add another one. I sometimes view my life as a checking account. It is solely my responsibility to keep my account in balance. However, at the end of the accounting period, if I am a little short, Christ will balance the account through his grace, and I will be okay. But I'd better not be way overdrawn, or off, or those judging my earthly acts will determine that I really haven't done enough. If that is the case, I will eventually need to make up the difference. If I make up the difference, I will still have to move to another neighborhood—one that I can better afford, given my income. So in this analogy, grace is simply the 'additional cash' deposited to balance my account: while I still have to earn most of the money myself and keep the account very close to being balanced."

From the back of the room we hear a gentle "amen" from someone who thinks that these analogies have pretty well told the story of grace.

About this time, Brother David Bradley, the stake patriarch, a well-grounded gospel leader and teacher, raises his hand. We notice people actually leaning toward him in order to catch everything he says.

"I have heard illustrations like these before. In fact, I have probably made some up. When I try to use illustrations to make a point, I usually use something I am familiar with, as the class members have this morning. We need to be careful, however, to not let the illustrations become the doctrine.

"Now," he says, "I want to say this respectfully, but there
is some risk in our attempts to simplify a complex doctrine
by making these simple comparisons of the Atonement being
like gravity, or a marathon, or our checking accounts. In fact,
I think that there are two unfortunate effects which may
come from ideas like the ones we've heard this morning. The
first may occur if we accept these illustrations as expressing
the whole meaning of the Atonement or grace. This is because we are frequently left with the feeling that 'this is impossible'—I can never do enough, I can't run long enough, or
I can't earn enough to qualify for help at the end. Such a conclusion is made a little more troubling when we discover that
the word *earn* does not appear even one time in the entire
Doctrine and Covenants! Doesn't that seem remarkable?

"Now, if I may continue," this perceptive elderly gentle-
man requests, "there is another conclusion, equally insidious,
which sadly might be drawn from these analogies. If we believe that it is all up to us, then during periods when we may
be having success—at least from our own perspective—we
might feel that we are solely responsible for the eternal result.
It is possible that we feel that we are achieving the steps of
salvation on our own, and we may think we are a bit better
than the others who don't seem to be doing as well. Stated
simply, *we feel we are doing it ourselves!*

"Now," he concludes gently, "I don't know if any of you
have ever had feelings like these, but I have. Frankly, I'm not
comfortable with either extreme. So I for one think that there
must be some other answer."

Gary Pulsipher, a newlywed, then blurts out, "Well,
Brother Bradley, if the analogies don't work, then what *is* the
answer?"

Wisely, the old patriarch defers, saying, "I would like to
know if others of our class have similar thoughts, or different
ones."

"That's a good question," says Brother Thomas, the instructor. "Does anyone else have a thought to add?"

With that encouragement, two class members raise their
hands. Max Adamson, a new grandfather, seems rather anxious to comment, so Brother Thomas calls on him first.

"When I was younger," he begins, "I really believed some of the ideas presented in the analogies discussed today. I really believed that my condition in the hereafter would be largely a result of my performance. As a youngster—during my teen years, for example—I didn't miss a church meeting from the time I was ordained a deacon in the Aaronic Priesthood until I was ordained an elder seven years later. I had 100 percent attendance at all my sacrament services, Sunday School meetings, priesthood meetings, and mutual activities.

"Some of you may remember that I grew up in Texas, and even in my somewhat remote stake just outside of Dallas, this was a time in the history of the Aaronic Priesthood program when special 'Individual Awards' were given for attendance at meetings. I was very motivated by these awards. I don't know how it was for you who grew up in other places, but in my home ward, these awards were presented in sacrament services in front of everyone. The award itself was a special printed certificate with assorted seals that symbolized varying levels of attendance.

"Additional recognition," he continues, "was frequently given for those who had attended 100 percent of their meetings. For example, one year all those who had 100 percent attendance in our ward were taken on a two-week trip to Canada. Another year I received a triple combination for my attendance. The following year I received a leather-bound missionary Bible. All of these were a result of my 100 percent attendance.

"I'm sure you will all understand that this type of motivation was probably useful because, at least for me, it helped develop positive habits and discipline that affect my life today. Nonetheless, I think that for me, this focus also contributed to the development of a belief that the gospel was centered in my works, my efforts, and my individual achievements.

"Now," he concludes wistfully, "I'm not so sure how to balance the concepts of my works and his grace."

The teacher, not one to push along too fast, gently asks Brother Adamson, "Max, what happened to cause you to change your mind?"

"Well," he replies, "it started about twenty or twenty-five years ago. Most of you know that I served as bishop when my wife, Karen, and I were quite a bit younger. What you may not know is that this service occurred when I was going to graduate school full time while also working to support our family. I didn't really feel that my efforts were all that herculean then, but looking back on it now, I don't know where my energy came from.

"Seriously," he adds, "I just felt that I was doing what most young men in their thirties did. We were working as hard as we knew how in order to provide for our families— both for the present and for the future.

"Anyway, one morning during my thirty-minute drive to school, I found myself reflecting on my time-demanding responsibilities as bishop, father, student, and employee. I was filled with feelings of inadequacy and guilt. I simply couldn't do it all, and I was tired of feeling guilty. I remember thinking that it wasn't fair that I was working that hard, only to feel guilty and to ultimately go to hell too. Then a comforting and powerful feeling swept over my heart that seemed to say, *I'm not critical of you. The criticism comes from within you. Your work is acceptable to me.* For the next couple of years this warm and tender feeling calmed the anxiety caused by my feeling that I could not do everything that I should do."

Mary Wilson, anxious to participate, asks directly, "So, Max, how do you feel now?"

"That's just it," he responds thoughtfully. "I know that I don't believe in works alone as strongly as I used to. That is to say, I don't feel as strongly that it all depends on me while I'm here on Earth. Even so, I'm not sure what the balance is between grace and works."

Sister Wilson then takes over the conversation, but no one minds. She has recently been released as a Gospel Doctrine teacher and is highly respected. She is a returned missionary and is married to Tom, who spoke earlier. They are the parents of four daughters, all teenagers. Her service as course instructor was outstanding. Everyone loves to listen to her illustrations.

As she begins, she refers to her college days just before

her mission. "My first exposure to the concept of grace caused me to view it suspiciously. As I was preparing for my mission to Tennessee, I attended an institute class in which the instructor told us about a missionary experience of his. His name was Brother Anderson, and he was a marvelous teacher.

"Brother Anderson spoke of two missionaries he knew who had been invited to speak to a congregation of fundamentalist Protestants. This was a group of faithful and wonderful people who believed in salvation by the profession of faith. Simply put, they believed—as many Protestants presently do—that salvation is available to any who accept Christ as their Savior. All that needs to be done is to verbally accept him, and heaven is assured. Though this is frequently accompanied by strong emotional experiences, the basic idea is a simple, vocal expression of faith . . . and that is all that is required for a person to go to heaven."

Continuing, Sister Wilson adds, "From my memory of his relating this story, Brother Anderson told us that the missionaries were asked to speak to this group who believed in salvation by grace only. Because the missionaries knew of the 'cheap grace' notion accepted by this congregation, they focused their remarks on scriptures illustrated by James chapter two, verses 17 through 20. If you don't mind, I'll quickly read these verses: 'Even so faith, if it hath not works, is dead, being alone. Yea, a man may say, Thou hast faith, and I have works: shew me thy faith without thy works, and I will shew thee my faith by my works. Thou believest that there is one God; thou doest well: the devils also believe, and tremble. But wilt thou know, O vain man, that faith without works is dead?'"

Finishing the reading, Sister Wilson adds, "Now, when the missionaries concluded their sermons on works, a member of the congregation was called upon to pray. His prayer was a simple one, and as the story went, he merely said, 'O Lord, we thank thee for Ephesians 2, verses 8 and 9. Amen.' After this unusually brief prayer, the entire congregation said an emphatic, 'Amen!'"

"Remind us, Mary—what do those verses say?" Brother Thomas queries.

"Well, Brother Anderson read them, and they have been indelibly engraved in my mind ever since. Paul states: 'For by grace are ye saved through faith; and that not of yourselves: it is the gift of God: not of works, lest any man should boast.'"

"Now," she continues, "Brother Anderson, our institute teacher telling the story of these missionaries, was undoubtedly familiar with this passage in Ephesians, and also with other passages of scripture concerning the Atonement, mercy, and grace. This familiarity no doubt gave him a balanced understanding of the relationship of justice and mercy, as well as grace and works. What I got out of the discussion that day was that grace was something that the Protestants believe, while we simply believe in works.

"In the class where the story was being told, Paul's statement was explained as a reference negating the 'dead works' of the law, not our necessary works in the gospel of Jesus Christ today. This explanation was given notwithstanding that the verse was written to the Ephesians and others who were primarily gentile converts to Christianity, and not merely to former Jews who had been converted to Christianity.

"Nevertheless," she continues, "I set aside this powerful observation of Paul, and concluded that his words referred to the works of the dead law of Moses and were not applicable to us today. I felt I must work out my own salvation by myself, alone, and with little help. This experience, along with others like it, strengthened my focus on individual performance of tasks in my Church service.

"One final thought," she concludes. "I feel I should emphatically add that I am *not* at all advocating that works are unnecessary. I am only saying that my personal emphasis on works in my younger years was out of balance. Such an approach left me with an inaccurate understanding of the true nature of the Atonement and of his grace that attends it."

You could tell by the reaction from the class members that many were puzzled by the thoughts that had been discussed thus far. Several hands went up, but Brother Thomas did not entertain any more comments. Instead, he indicated that because time was growing short, he would like to move on. Doing so, he asked the group to help him create two lists.

"On one side of the blackboard," he begins, "let's list words or phrases with perhaps a scripture or two that seem to emphasize works, and then on the other side let's do the same with grace."

After a few minutes, the blackboard looked something like this:

WORKS	GRACE
- justice - punishment - achievement - credit 2 Nephi 25:23 after all we can do D&C 130:20–21 law irrevocably decreed Jacob 1:19 labored diligently to rid garments of blood of sinners Alma 42:25 mercy cannot rob justice	- mercy - encircled in the arms of his love - the tender mercies of the Lord 2 Nephi 26:25 come and buy milk and honey *without money* and *without price* 2 Nephi 10:24 after reconciled, only through grace of God that we're saved 2 Nephi 2:4 salvation is free

As they finished the lists, Brother Thomas noted that the time had passed; and while indicating that the class must be dismissed, he concluded with this thought: "I know that there are still many unresolved feelings here today. Why don't we continue considering this topic next week?"

He then gave some assignments, bore a brief but tender testimony, and invited Sister Runyon to pray.

For now, let's step back outside of that Gospel Doctrine classroom. Perhaps we'll visit this class a little later to see how the class progresses in their examination of the doctrine of grace. In the meantime, consider the effects of an over-emphasis on individual performance. In the gospel context, such behavior may well lead to our forgetting the One who set all things in motion to lead us back to our heavenly home. Don had an experience that underscores the possible impact of failing to understand the relationship of the Atonement, grace, and our works. He shares it as the next chapter unfolds.

_____Notes

1. Bruce R. McConkie, "The Purifying Power of Gethsemane," *Ensign*, May 1985, p. 10.

CHAPTER THREE

The 'Mormon Church' or the Church of Jesus Christ?

Not long ago I (Don) was traveling from British Columbia to Boston by way of Salt Lake. The stop in Salt Lake was brief, as I simply had to change planes. I was one of the first on board, so I quickly found my customary aisle seat and started to get settled. Because the seat beside me, the window seat, was vacant, it looked as though it would be a comfortable five-hour flight home. There would be time for reading, some quiet reflection, and maybe a little nap.

Just before takeoff, a polite young man tapped me on the shoulder. "Hi," he said. "My name's Alan. Do you mind if I take the seat next to you?"

Honestly, I almost wanted to say, "No, please find a seat in the back, as I want to sit here in quiet comfort." But Alan was holding a boarding pass which indicated that the window seat was his, so I didn't. Instead, I said what I should have; I invited him to sit down. I then stood up to make the entrance easier for him.

I let my new flight companion know that I was originally from Salt Lake City, but that now I lived in the East. Further, I indicated that I had family in Utah and that I spent a lot of time in the state. Alan said that he was from San Diego and was on his way to Maine to do some fly-fishing with his brother.

The flight attendant soon announced that we were preparing for takeoff. Moments later, as the plane lifted off the runway, the two of us engaged in a few more minutes of small talk; then we both settled into the monotony of the flight. I no sooner began to read something of interest, when I noticed Alan reading the New Testament. In fact, he was studying the book of Thessalonians. Why, I wondered, would anyone choose to study Thessalonians? Everyone knows that it is difficult to understand, and that there are absolutely no pictures in it.

But my curiosity was piqued, so I asked, "Are you a theologian, Alan?"

"Are you a Mormon?" was his response.

"Yes, I am," I replied, somewhat surprised. "Are you?"

"No," he replied honestly, "but I work closely with several Mormons—five of them, actually."

What followed was a nearly nonstop discussion on a five-hour flight across the United States. I told Alan that I had been studying the doctrine of grace with a lot of intensity lately, and that I was excited to share ideas with a Protestant who was a student of the New Testament. As it turned out, Alan told me that he was a lay minister of a small Protestant group, and he welcomed the opportunity to try to save another "misguided" Mormon. So we were well matched!

I should add that Alan knew his scriptures as if he'd been born to them. After visiting for an hour or so, he indicated that he would like to pose a question. In framing it, he said that he had asked all of his Mormon coworkers a similar question. He wondered how I would respond.

"Suppose," Alan began, "that I came as a first-time visitor to your church. Following the meetings, I tell you I have a question for you. My question is, what must I do to go to heaven?"

Alan indicated further that as my fictional visiting guest, he was not very familiar with the Holy Bible—he had not really studied it much, nor had he regularly attended church.

Now, I have to admit that I had a hunch where Alan was going with his question, so I answered it in New Testament terms. "Well," I replied, "you would have to come to an understanding of the atonement of the Lord Jesus Christ, exercise faith in him by accepting him as your Savior, and then repent of your sins and follow his teachings."

Alan was surprised at my answer. His next comment was troubling. He indicated that he had asked each of his Mormon coworkers a similar question. After the seemingly most well informed of the group had responded, Alan had said to this coworker, "You have spoken for forty-five minutes, yet you have not even mentioned Jesus Christ. I have learned about three heavens, Joseph Smith, the Book of Mormon, the importance of keeping commandments and doing good works, but I have not learned anything about the role of Jesus Christ. He must not have an important place in your church."

Even in light of this rather direct criticism, the response Alan heard from his coworker was not an apology followed by a fearless defense of Christ's position in The Church of Jesus Christ of Latter-day Saints. I pressed to know what exactly the response had been. Alan told me his Mormon friend seemed to say that while Christ had an important role to play in the Mormon church, it was not a central role in relation to our salvation. He was told that we must work out our salvation by ourselves, or words to that effect.

As Alan finished relating this experience, he said, "You, on the other hand, are a peculiar Mormon! I have never met a 'Biblical Mormon' before. You've spent much time talking about Christ, and you've used the New Testament as your text. I've never heard a Mormon testify of the Savior as you have. Tell me truthfully—are you a renegade Mormon?"

No, I'm not a "Mormon" at all, I thought without saying it. *I belong to the Church of Jesus Christ, and I am doing what I know how to do to become a disciple of the Master.*

But, my thoughts continued, *if that is so, why do I not testify of him more often? Why do I speak in meetings and sometimes never say his name except when I close my talk "in the name of Jesus Christ"? How can I ever bear testimony in another testimony meeting and not bear witness of him?*

My spoken answer to Alan, however, was simply that I was not a renegade Mormon, but one who was becoming more aware of the importance of the Savior in my life. But I also knew that had Alan asked me his original question before I had begun my study of the Book of Mormon and of the Savior, I may well have answered him just like his coworkers had done.

This conversation went on for several hours, and I have tried to summarize much of it in just a few short paragraphs. Now let me finish the story. After the plane landed, Alan and I disembarked together; and after a brief exchange of good-byes we went our separate ways.

Lest someone think this is an isolated experience, let me add another. After I shared this story about Alan with a friend, my friend gave me a copy of a talk given at Brigham Young University in 1993 by Elder Dallin H. Oaks.[1] In this talk, which Elder Oaks referred to as the most important he had ever given on the campus of Brigham Young University, he discussed in detail the need of Latter-day Saints to testify more frequently of Christ. He spoke of a letter he received from a man who had outlined a simple survey he had taken in ward meetings. The man indicated that on a particular fast Sunday, seventeen people bore their testimonies. Not one testified of Christ. Additionally, the man reported that the following week not one of seven sacrament service speakers spoke or testified of Christ. Neither did this man hear the Savior's name mentioned in the Gospel Doctrine class or the priesthood quorum meeting.

Anticipating those who might question whether such behavior was widespread in the Church, Elder Oaks indicated that while such conduct may not have been universal, it was certainly all too common.

After I read Elder Oaks's talk, I decided to listen for the same thing in the Church meetings I attended. Actually, I must confess that I knew from experience what I would find out. The following fast Sunday I heard twenty-one people bear testimony in a testimony meeting—including five children being prompted by their parents. It was a good meeting, and the testimonies of the children were especially sweet and tender. Not one of these twenty-one testimonies, however, were centered on Christ; and not one of the children even mentioned Christ except in closing.

I found it particularly troubling that these little children were learning by modeling the testimonies of my generation. Could it be true that we aren't teaching our children to bear witness of Christ? If we don't help them see the Savior's central role in our salvation, how will they learn of it? Could it be that we don't testify of him because we really don't appreciate or understand what he does for us?

Brent and I are certainly not suggesting that the above scenario is true churchwide, but we know that in our own families we have not testified of Christ and the power of the Atonement as often as we should have.

Even so, the experiences of visiting with Alan on the plane, reading Elder Oaks's talk, and having many conversations with friends have driven us to approach this whole topic differently. We will try to never again give a talk or present a lesson without mentioning our Savior. We are also committed to never stand to share a testimony and not bear witness of the power of the Atonement and of our appreciation for the grace of Christ and the Father. We will also try to make sure that when a nonmember asks about our church, we will leave no doubt in his or her mind that The Church of Jesus Christ of Latter-day Saints is a Christian church dedicated to following the Savior's teachings.

We will try to follow the implied admonition of Nephi when he said, "And we talk of Christ, we rejoice in Christ, we preach of Christ, we prophesy of Christ, and we write according to our prophecies, that our children may know to what source they may look for a remission of their sins" (2 Nephi 25:26).

_____NOTES

1. See Dallin H. Oaks, "'Another Testament of Jesus Christ,'" in *Brigham Young University 1992–93 Devotional and Fireside Speeches* (Provo, Utah: University Publications, 1993), pp. 111–22.

The Study of Doctrine
Changes Behavior

What we have attempted to describe in the first three chapters is a series of related events. Though they were not necessarily related in time, they are related in concept. We have sought to illustrate the beginning of a discovery that took us several years to recognize. Over a period of time we are gaining a more complete and accurate understanding of some of the basic concepts regarding Christ's mission. As we reviewed our own growth—which is definitely work in progress—we are humbled to realize that our understanding of the doctrines of grace and the Atonement has expanded. Thinking back on that growth, we tried to assess the process in which we have been involved.

A mutual friend related to us a story that seems to illustrate an important point to help us describe that process. He told us that, while serving as a stake president, he attended a gathering of the stake presidents in his area. At the meeting a visiting General Authority asked those attending to identify the greatest problems in their respective stakes. They gave such answers as apathy, immorality, and so forth.

This visiting authority then taught them that these types of problems were problems of behavior. He further indicated that as leaders and teachers in the Church, they should address those problems by teaching principles from the scriptures and from the doctrines of the Church. To summarize, he reportedly said, "The study of doctrine will do more to affect behavior than the study of behavior."

Sometime after we heard the description of that meeting, we learned that Elder Boyd K. Packer taught these ideas in a general conference address. Elder Packer said: "True doctrine, understood, changes attitudes and behavior. The study of the doctrines of the gospel will improve behavior quicker than a study of behavior will improve behavior. Preoccupation with unworthy behavior can lead to unworthy behavior. That is why we stress so forcefully the study of the doctrines of the gospel."[1]

We knew this was true because our studying of the Atonement by reading the Book of Mormon had begun to influence and change our attitudes and behavior. As we have contemplated the process of change and tried to explain it to others, we haven't always been successful. So we have developed a visual representation of a process that we believe people go through when they properly study the doctrine of the kingdom. As we look back on the growth of our own understanding of Christ's mission, his atonement, and the doctrine of grace, we find that we went through a process like this:

Pattern of Spiritual Discovery and Growth

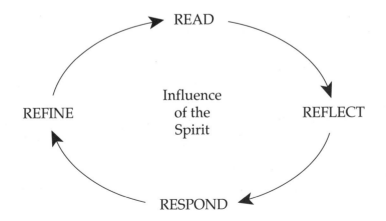

In this model, the cycle repeats itself to illustrate that it is both repetitive and continuous. We grow in our understanding of the doctrines of the gospel by either *reading* about them or by listening to others speak about them. Then, by thinking about or *reflecting* upon what we have read or heard, we gain new insights into the gospel. These insights usually entail a necessary behavior change, and so we *respond* to what we have learned by doing the actions suggested or required by the doctrine. Finally, the experiences which come from working with our new perceptions help us *refine* our understanding of the things we have been learning. Throughout, the process is influenced by the Holy Spirit, without which no significant discoveries of spiritual truths will occur.

Among the things that can frustrate this process is a failure to read and study the doctrines of the kingdom. For example, when we don't study we may be left to reflect solely upon discussions from classes we attend or conversations with our acquaintances. If these discussions are not based upon sound doctrine, we are left to respond to inaccurate doctrine. This, of course, will lead to incorrect conclusions and faulty behavior. Reading and studying the doctrine of the kingdom, therefore, is an essential step in our eternal progression.

We might add that one of the reasons why it is imperative that teachers find and teach true doctrine is so that students will not be hindered in their progress because of our failure to teach the truth.

Our model of growth and behavioral change could be seen as continuous and not intermittent. In other words, because most of us are considering a variety of gospel topics at any given time, we could be at several or all of the points on a given day. In gospel study and living among the faithful, wonderful discoveries and significant changes eventually occur, possibly through a process like that described above. Because it is true that some of our own personal discoveries came from a process like this one, we wanted to describe it before we continued so that you would be able to see the pattern as we see it and understand better where we are headed in this book.

If you look at the table of contents you will see that it is outlined in a pattern similar to the model. That is:

—Part 1, "A Change of Mind," refers to step one, *read.*
—Part 2, "A Change of Heart," refers to step two, *reflect.*
—Part 3, "A Change of Behavior," refers to step three, *respond.*
—Part 4, "A Change of Perspective," refers to step four, *refine.*

In fact, the material contained herein is presented largely in the order of our discovery and turns out to be parallel to the steps shown in the model. It is clear to us that when one of the steps is left out, confusion or frustration often occurs.

As with any model or representation of human behavior, this one is a simplified version of a complex process. However, we do feel it makes the process easier to understand. We have found this visualization of a change process useful, and hope you do as well.

_____NOTES

1. Boyd K. Packer, in Conference Report, October 1986, p. 20.

PART 2

A Change of Heart:
Feeling Christ's Tender
Mercies and Grace

W_e (Don and Brent) have been talking and we think that most of you who are reading this did fairly well with the hypothetical Gospel Doctrine class we presented earlier. So we're going to introduce you to another group and let you listen in on their discussion. We ask that you remember that this group won't know you are here with them, so don't be too loud as you turn the next several pages. If you are, you may give away our secret and we won't be able to sneak around like this again.

Let's look in on a New England institute class. It's a typical Thursday night, and the instructor is just standing up to greet the class. The setting is the institute in the outskirts of Boston, Massachusetts. Between the undergraduate and graduate institute courses he teaches, Brother Terrance Matthews has a lot to do. He is the only full-time instructor assigned there, which really is a challenge. Why, with his early-morning seminary supervision and his full load of institute courses—both morning and evening classes—he sometimes feels swamped. Of course, he does love his work, and thus takes the pressure in stride.

We're now going to slip into the back of the room in one of his evening classes. He is just getting started. Oh, one other thing—while the characters and location are fictional, the story the instructor is about to tell is true, incredible as that may seem.

"Now, class," Brother Matthews begins following the prayer, "as you know, we're making real progress through the Book of Mormon. Our attention has often been drawn to the doctrines of the gospel related to the Atonement. Tonight let's start with a verse in Alma 32—verse 21. While the topic here might be faith or hope, I want to discuss how Alma's def-initions might apply when we study any gospel principle. But first let's read the passage."

Brother Matthews turns to Kiki Smith, an undergraduate student in chemical engineering. "Kiki, would you mind reading slowly Alma 32:21? As you finish the verse, tell us what you think Alma is saying."

Kiki opens to the passage and begins: " 'And now as I said concerning faith—faith is not to have a perfect knowl-edge of things; therefore if ye have faith ye hope for things which are not seen, which are true.'

"Well," she starts after a brief pause, "it's clear that Alma is saying a couple of things. I can see that he says uncertainty of information or understanding has to be there in order for faith to exist. Also, it seems faith and hope are closely inter-twined."

"Do you think he is saying anything else?" Brother Matthews asks encouragingly.

"Well, I think he is also telling us that faith and hope must be exercised on the truth, not fiction. Now, Brother Matthews," she adds, "I don't claim to know what all of that means, but that's what Alma seems to be saying."

"Very good, Kiki, and really not too bad for someone who spends her days in a laboratory," Brother Matthews interjects cheerfully. He then continues, "Actually, it is Alma's last phrase that I want to discuss. Do you see that if the object of our faith is not truth, then it is not really faith but only belief."

Going on, he says, "Now, you all know me well enough to know that I can't get too far into a topic without telling a story. So as not to disappoint you, let's try this one.

"This story used to be a true story from my youth. I'll try to keep it all factual, but probably by this time, twenty-five or thirty years later, a little color has slipped in. In this case it really doesn't matter, because I simply want to use the story as a metaphor. Let's see if you can discover the meaning as I see it.

"This story goes back about forty years—"

"Wait a minute," someone exclaims from the back of the room. "You just said twenty-five to thirty years, and it changed to forty years in less than a minute."

"Well, I was checking to see who was listening," Brother Matthews responds. "Now, going back a long, long time to when I was in Primary . . . Will you all accept that?" The class laughs and nods in agreement, so he goes ahead with the story.

"At that time, our stake in Idaho regularly sponsored an annual Articles of Faith convention. All the Primary children in the stake ages nine to eleven were invited to attend. It was held in our stake center each spring, and we were always eager to attend.

"Anyway, after some opening exercises we were divided into small groups and sent with a teacher into one of the classrooms. The goal was for each child to have memorized a certain number of the Articles of Faith, depending on their age, and then on this day to recite those to the assigned teacher. Nine-year-olds were to know five articles of faith, ten-year-olds were to know ten of them, and the eleven-year-olds were to know all thirteen.

"Needless to say," he laughs honestly, "with my competitive drive, every year I was determined to learn and repeat all thirteen! After all, there was a certificate and some public recognition for those who achieved the most. At the first two conventions I accomplished this feat, received my certificate of award, and went home well satisfied.

"When I went to the convention for the last time, it was just after my eleventh birthday. I recited all thirteen articles, just as I had the previous year. This time, however, I volunteered to be first, and was then allowed to leave the room and find the refreshments. As I walked out into the hallway, I met two girls I knew from school. We talked for a few minutes and then as I walked away, they began following me. I wasn't comfortable with that, so I walked faster—they picked up their pace. Pretty soon I was running away from them and they were running too. I have to admit, it was a little flattering."

Smiling mischievously, Brother Matthews then adds, "A lot of people may wonder what the girls could have possibly seen in me; but of course, that was before the accident . . ."

Some in the class smile, and two or three in the room even snicker. One of the students comments, "Come on,

Brother Matthews, you know there wasn't an accident. Why, you've always looked like this!"

"I know, I know," Brother Matthews responds. "But remember, adding a little color isn't too bad. Now, let me go back to the hostile pursuit."

With a little encouragement from the class, he continues. "As I made my way helter-skelter away from the girls, I came to a stairway. The girls were gaining on me, which was in and of itself a bit embarrassing; but I explained it away by reminding myself that their two purses were quite heavy.

"You don't suppose that the fact I stole their purses had anything to do with their chasing me, do you?" he asks with feigned innocence. Without waiting for a response, he adds, "No, I don't think so either.

"Anyway, to increase my chances of getting away from them, I leaped up several stairs and bounded to the top. There were no lights on in the hallway, but I had been in the building several times before, and I remembered a room about halfway back. *Why,* I said to myself, *I can run down the hall, dart into the room, hide in the back, and they'll never find me. They'll become frightened because of the dark, and turn back.*

"As I came to the point in the hall where the room was, I remembered that I needed to turn and go down a pitch-black hallway to the doorway of the room. So I quickly made the turn and ran toward the doorway when, to my surprise, I learned that this was *not* a hallway, but a *stairwell!* I raced out into thin air, thinking my feet would continue to make contact with the floor. There was no floor, however, only stairs; and before I realized what was happening, I plummeted to the bottom landing."

There are some incredulous gasps from around the classroom, but without stopping to reply, Brother Matthews continues with great excitement.

"Wrapped in a ball of arms, legs, body, and purses, I rolled until I came to a door at the bottom of the stairs— which, I might add, was unfortunately closed. I truthfully slammed into the door with a loud thud.

"Moments later, class, the door opened partway. The girls were standing at the top of the stairs and had turned on the light. They could see the results of my swan dive, and they were *laughing*, if you can believe that! The person on the other side of the partly opened door was the building custodian.

" 'What are you doing here?' he asked.

" 'I just fell down this stairwell,' I responded somewhat painfully.

" 'Well, don't ever do it again!' he growled, and closed the door with a bang.

"As the door was closing, I promised that I would never repeat my transgression of trying to break the law of gravity."

An empathetic student then blurts out, "Were you hurt, Brother Matthews, or were you just frightened?"

"More frightened than anything," he replies, "but I *was* hurting! Sometime later, long after the bruises, bumps, and embarrassment had healed, I began to ponder the significance of what had happened. Upon reflection, I realized that I believed, without question, that the stairwell was a hallway. Even so, my strong belief did not keep me suspended in the air—even for a moment.

"Now," says the teacher, "I think there are some true principles here. I wonder if anyone in class can see what I'm getting at."

Several students make comments, at the conclusion of which Carol Tenneson, an undergraduate student from San Diego, says, "Well, I think it is only faith when it is directed towards things that are true. Strong belief—even without a shadow of a doubt—does not change the truth, even if I'm a strong, active, believing member."

Ralph Maddox adds without raising his hand, "From what I see, Brother Matthews, as a boy at that convention, you learned the truth of Alma's statement 'If ye have faith ye hope for things which are not seen, *which are true.'*"

"Very good," Brother Matthews responds. "Both of those comments are excellent. Can anyone see a connection among this story, what Carol and Ralph have just said, and our discussion about the meaning of the Atonement?"

"Well," Adam Richards volunteers, "I think you are trying to help us see the importance of believing the truth about the Atonement and of not being satisfied with a lack of diligent study on the topic."

Before Brother Matthews can comment, Connie Walston interjects, "As I think of your experience in light of the Atonement, I can see the importance of believing and acting upon the truth. Now, Brother Matthews, I also understand a little better why you had encouraged us to become familiar with the quotation you used last Thursday from Elder Bruce R. McConkie. I've got it here in my notes, so I want to read it. Concerning the Atonement, Elder McConkie said, 'But if we are to have faith like Enoch and Elijah we must believe what they believed, know what they knew, and live as they lived.'"[1]

Brother Matthews then adds, "It is satisfying to see that many of you are really getting the point. I am very motivated by Elder McConkie's talk, particularly the excerpt that Connie read. I have a determined desire to know what those prophets knew and believe what they believed, that I may one day live as they lived. I think we should all want to possess an accurate understanding of the Atonement. Now, next week we're going to talk about grace as it relates to the Atonement and the mission of Christ."

The class concludes with some further discussion about the relationship of faith and truth.

_____NOTES

1. Bruce R. McConkie, "The Purifying Power of Gethsemane," *Ensign*, May 1985, p. 10.

CHAPTER FIVE

His Tender Mercies:
Discovering and Defining Grace

It's hard for us to believe that an entire week has passed since we last looked in on the Gospel Doctrine class. You may remember that they finished the class period without really reaching any conclusions on their discussion regarding grace. Brother Randy Thomas has decided to continue the discussion about grace and has asked some specific class members to come prepared to respond to questions that he gave them during the week. Let's listen in, albeit very quietly.

Brother Thomas opens the class discussion in this manner: "Brothers and sisters, if I were to say to you that as a member of The Church of Jesus Christ of Latter-day Saints I believe I am saved by grace, how would you react?"

Tom Wilson quickly replies, "Salvation could mean to be resurrected; so, because all are resurrected, with the only requirement being that we be born here on earth, I suppose that with that strict definition your statement would be acceptable to me."

Brother Thomas responds by saying, "While a common idea associated with the word *salvation* is resurrection, in almost all cases the scriptural use of the term is exaltation. Elder Bruce R. McConkie taught this fact in his book *Mormon Doctrine,* but if you wonder, you might check it out in your own scriptures. It is clearly true. Assuming, for the purposes of our discussion, that salvation and exaltation are synonyms and that, as I said, I believe I am saved or exalted by grace, how would you respond?"

"Well," Brother Wilson replies honestly, "if by that you mean you are saved by grace only, I would have trouble with the statement."

"Without avoiding answering this question more fully right now, would you agree that in order to find the answer, we need to define terms carefully?" Brother Thomas inquires. Answering his own question, he states, "Our subject again today is grace. You should remember that we left class last week with some unfinished business. There were many opinions about the role of grace in our salvation or exaltation. We heard some express with analogies their feeling that they believed their eternal future largely depends on their efforts. They were suggesting that their works will be the most significant factor in the determination of where they end up. Others, while acknowledging the importance of individual labor, were not so sure.

"Today, to help us get a better sense of the truth of the matter, I thought that perhaps we should consider some definitions. You may recall that we had these items on the chalkboard at the end of last week's lesson."

Brother Thomas pauses, and turns around the portable chalkboard to reveal a duplication of the previous week's list.

"Now," Brother Thomas continues, "I want to start today with a few questions. First of all, let's use a second chalkboard and work on a definition of grace. Who would like to start?"

Toni Adamson, Max Adamson's wife and also a new grandmother, raises her hand and says, "Max and I talked about grace off and on during the week. We looked in the dictionary and through the scriptures and came to the conclusion that grace is an unearned, perhaps even an unearnable gift."

As Toni speaks, Brother Thomas writes her words on the permanent blackboard attached to the wall behind him. "That's a very good start, Toni," he replies. "What do the rest of you think? Is her definition complete?"

"I don't think so," volunteers Connie Hart. "It seems that there has to be more to it."

"What would you suggest?" Brother Thomas inquires, adding, "Give me something to put up here on the board."

"Well," Sister Hart continues, "I think it has to show the intent of the giver and the response of the one who receives the gift. With that in mind, I think that the gift is freely given without expectation from the one giving it. And the gift is received without obligation from the one who accepts it. Otherwise, of course, it is not a gift."

"I'll try to put that on the board," Brother Thomas interjects warmly. "Tell me if I get it right." He adds to the sentence he started writing previously, separating the elements of the statement to allow the class members to more clearly examine each portion of it:

GRACE

An unearned gift which is

freely given without expectation
on the part of the one giving it

AND

which is accepted gratefully by the recipient
but without further obligation

otherwise it is not a gift

"Brothers and sisters," says Brother Thomas, "here is an attempt to define the word *grace* without making reference to how it applies in the gospel context. Any comments?"

"Could we add a few synonyms and characteristics of the word *grace*, please?" asks Anna Dilworth. Anna, a longtime member of the ward, is a real class favorite and someone we will hear more from in a later discussion. Those present affectionately call her Sister Anna.

"That's a good idea, Sister Anna," Brother Thomas responds courteously. "Do you have any suggestions?"

"The word *favor* comes to mind," replies Sister Dilworth. "By this I mean a condition of being 'in his favor.' It is a positive condition in a relationship, not just doing a favor for someone else." She continues, "I think it is important to realize that grace is not a single event. It is maybe a process or a condition."

"Well, Sister Anna, let's write some of those ideas down."

A moment later, as Brother Thomas finishes writing, the board looks like this:

GRACE*

An unearned gift which is

freely given without expectation
on the part of the one giving it

AND

which is accepted gratefully by the recipient but
without further obligation

otherwise it is not a gift

SYNONYMS and CHARACTERISTICS
Favor, like "in his favor"
Not an event
More like a process or condition

Authors' note: This is a simplified attempt to start a definition of grace. Clearly, it is unfinished. Our goal throughout the balance of this book is to allow the definition to evolve. No reader should assume that this initial attempt is even close to being complete. In the coming chapters, some ideas shown here are dropped and others enlarged until a more complete definition is attained. However, a final definition of grace is not found herein. We, the authors, continue to grow in our understanding of the Lord's infinite expressions of love for all his children.

"Now," he says while turning to the class, "we're running out of space here, so let's stop and talk about this. Remember, we're not trying to come up with a complete, last and forever definition. We're just looking for a good place to start. Now, are there any other comments?"

Tom Wilson, who gave the analogy about gravity last week, immediately shoots up his hand and declares, "If this refers to salvation by grace and grace alone, I think we're way off base."

"Now, Tom," David Bradley, the patriarch, inserts quickly but calmly, "I think that's a swift judgment about the direction this discussion is going. The complexity of the meaning of the word *grace* makes it difficult to define. Let me add to Sister Anna's comments by pointing out other uses of the word. Those who find themselves 'in his grace' have unique access to the Savior. If we are found 'in the favor' of Christ and the Father, it means we have a special relationship with them. So, while grace may sometimes be thought of as an act, it is far more than that. Personally, I think this is why we are having difficulty coming up with an acceptable definition—one that satisfies everyone."

"Thanks, Brother Bradley," Brother Thomas replies honestly. "While I understand and share some of Tom's concerns, I appreciate these additional insights. We're making progress here, I think, and that's good. To add to our understanding, however, I thought it would be useful to look for examples of grace in action in the scriptures. I've asked two of our class members who were here last week to help us. Becky, why don't you begin? Come to the front of the class, if you don't mind, so we can all hear what you have to say."

Becky Strong taught a Gospel Doctrine class for several years and has a reputation for her meticulous preparation. She is genuinely respected by those in the class as an excellent gospel scholar.

"My subject today is the Apostle Paul," she begins. "You no doubt remember that Paul was known as Saul prior to his conversion. As I looked into Saul's early history, I found that the book of Acts and his epistles are fairly quiet about his life before his conversion. The most important items seem to be as follows: First, he was a very strict practitioner of the Jewish faith. In fact, he identified himself as a Pharisee, the strictest sect of the Jewish religion. This information is found in Acts 26:5. Second, he was a passive participant in the stoning of Stephen. He apparently assented to his death. Third, he was so aggressive in his opposition toward the upstart followers of Christ that he pursued them from village to village and city to city.

"This zealous opposition to Christianity led Saul to take the road to Damascus, a city that is located about 150 miles northeast of Jerusalem, in Syria. It was while walking along this road that Saul met his Master for the first time. Seemingly out of nowhere came this call to follow the Savior. Saul listened and obeyed. I suppose that anyone who had been so singularly identified and plucked from the midst of antagonism toward the work of the Lord would have moments of deep reflection about his worthiness to be a part of it.

"Surely," Becky continues, sensing that she is connecting with the members of the class, "this was true of Saul, who was thereafter known as Paul. For example, he wrote of himself in 1 Corinthians chapter 15 verse 9, 'For I am the least of the apostles, that am not meet to be called an apostle, because I persecuted the church of God.' He goes on further to write in the following verse, 'But by the *grace* of God I am what I am: and his *grace* which was bestowed upon me was not in vain; but I laboured more abundantly than they all: yet not I, but the *grace of God which was with me.*'

"From only these few observations it is clear that Paul the Apostle had a unique appreciation for the grace of Christ. His writings are filled with discussions of Heavenly Father's tender mercies, or of his favor, as Sister Anna noted. In my opinion, it's unfair to the Apostle Paul to oversimplify his teachings by saying that every comment he makes about grace is in response to the Jewish reliance on the law of Moses. It seems clear to me that sometimes he was talking about the merciful response of a loving Father for his children.

"In fact," Becky concludes, "my studies this week have convinced me that Paul was saying in this passage from 1 Corinthians, and also in many other references that I studied this week, that his good efforts were possible only through the grace of the Lord. This is a significantly different idea than the one I had a few weeks ago, before these discussions began."

"Thank you, Becky," Brother Thomas replies while she takes her seat. "Though there may be comments or questions about Becky's presentation, I would like to wait until our next speaker, Gary Pulsipher, has given his presentation. Gary, would you please come up and tell what you prepared concerning Alma the Younger."

Gary has been in the ward only about six months. He has an infectious enthusiasm that seems to draw people to him, but the comments he gives today let others know a little more about the serious young man he is.

"Brothers and sisters," he begins, "I spent several hours this week looking at the passages of scripture written about and by Alma the Younger. His story begins in Mosiah 27 and doesn't end until Alma 45. This is 123 pages, or about one-fourth of the Book of Mormon. As we all know, young Alma was a prominent character and major contributor to the historical and doctrinal expressions of the Nephite records.

"These last few days," Gary continues, "I read this entire section of the Book of Mormon. Some of it I just skimmed over, but I reviewed every passage that contained specific references to Alma or his teachings. And I couldn't get away from the fact that there was an unusual intervention in Alma's life for which he was not directly responsible. When the angel appeared, he indicated—as you all may remember—that Alma's father and others had prayed in faith and that the heavenly visitation was in response to those prayers.

"From Alma's perspective, this manifestation was truly an act of grace. Alma the Younger always had his agency, his ability to choose, but the dramatic method by which the choice was placed before him was a gift from God.

"Now," Gary summarizes, "I don't want to leave the wrong impression. Alma's sermons and writings clearly outline his belief in the importance of our efforts in the eternal scheme of things. No one can read chapters 5, 36, or 41 through 43 of the book of Alma and not come away with an understanding that much of our salvation depends on us. But by the same token, it is clear that Alma's life and his teachings indicate his belief that the grace of Christ starts the process of conversion. As we then humble ourselves and accept him, his grace continues. Throughout our lives his grace is part of our efforts to do his work.

"In conclusion," Gary adds, "this exercise has been helpful for me. It has given me additional insights into the partnership that I have with Christ and Heavenly Father. As I think about my own life, I can see his many acts of grace—blessings which came to me as gifts, not earned in any way I can see—which have guided and directed my decisions. I am truly grateful for his tender mercies."

"That was excellent," says Brother Thomas. "Does anyone have anything else to add?" Seeing no response, he moves the discussion along. "Brothers and sisters, I believe that these episodes are significant expressions of the meaning of grace. If Paul were interviewed, he would surely talk about his conversion coming through the grace of Christ. If Alma the Younger were to discuss his miraculous conversion, I believe that he too would tell us that his life was forever changed—not by events of his own making, but rather, solely by the grace of our Savior and the concern of others. There are many scriptures in the words of both Paul and Alma that illustrate a deep and abiding gratitude for the tender mercies of the Lord.

"Now, moving on, I have asked several people to read some other material and comment on it. So let's go on to those who have these assignments. Max, would you tell us about Elder McConkie's talk."

Max Adamson stands and faces the group. "Randy asked me to read Elder Bruce R. McConkie's talk 'The Purifying Power of Gethsemane,' which was given at the April 1985 general conference. It was his final public address and, as you may recall, was a stirring tribute to the life and ministry of the Savior. It was also a reflection of Elder McConkie's lifetime study of the Christ. There is much in his talk for us to consider, but I will only point out these few paragraphs. He states: 'Now, the atonement of Christ is the most basic and

fundamental doctrine of the gospel, and it is the least understood of all our revealed truths.

" 'Many of us have a superficial knowledge and rely
upon the Lord and his goodness to see us through the trials
and perils of life.

" 'But if we are to have faith like Enoch and Elijah we
must believe what they believed, know what they knew, and
live as they lived.

" 'May I invite you to join with me in gaining a sound
and sure knowledge of the Atonement.

" 'We must cast aside the philosophies of men and the
wisdom of the wise and hearken to that Spirit which is given
to us to guide us into all truth.

" 'We must search the scriptures, accepting them as the
mind and will and voice of the Lord and the very power of
God unto salvation.'[1]

"Because these words have so much significance regarding
the topic which we have been discussing," Brother Adamson
continues, "I have typed these paragraphs on a handout for
each of you. As I read through this talk and thought about our
discussion from last week, I knew that I was one of those who
did not adequately understand the meaning of the Atonement.
You see, I knew that Elder McConkie was speaking to me. I
think I have placed too much emphasis on my own efforts and
not enough emphasis on what Christ has done—and continues to do—for me. This reading assignment has filled me with
a desire to more rigorously study the Atonement so that I may
develop a more complete and accurate understanding of it.
This is all I have to say." Max then quickly distributes the
handouts and sits down.

"Thank you, Max, for that stirring statement," Brother
Thomas replies softly. "Now, let's listen to what May has to
say."

Thirty-year-old May Dexter stands and begins. She is a
single mother whose life experiences have taught her much
about her assigned topic. "My assignment was to read
through Brother Bruce Hafen's book *The Broken Heart*.[2]
Actually, Brother Thomas just asked me to report on the introduction to the book, 'The Atonement Is Not Just for

Sinners.' I believe it originally appeared as an article in the *Ensign*. I was so moved by what Brother Hafen wrote in this article that I read the whole book, which I would recommend to everyone.

"My report is a simple one. I discovered something I must have always known—Christ did not suffer only for the sins of his people. As it says in Alma 7 verses 11 through 12, he suffered 'pains and afflictions and temptations of every kind . . . he [took] upon him the pains and the sicknesses of his people . . . and their infirmities, that his bowels may be filled with mercy, according to the flesh, that he may know according to the flesh how to succor his people according to their infirmities.'

"It should not surprise us to know that this remarkable description was written by Alma the Younger—one who knew something about the tender mercies of the Lord. Brother Hafen reintroduced me to the concepts expressed so richly in this and other passages—that Christ's atonement was not just for those who commit the 'big' sins. It was also for people like me. I learned that in addition to paying for my sins, he suffered so that he could understand and help me with my weaknesses, my failures, my oversights, and my sorrows. These ideas have forever changed my appreciation and understanding of the kindness and caring which come from him."

Sister Dexter then adds her testimony and sits down.

"Thank you so much, May. We have two other reports that we need to hear. Let's ask Richard Jackson to tell us about some of Robert Millet's writings. Richard?"

"Thanks, Randy," Richard replies as he stands up. "I read one of Brother Millet's books and looked through a couple of others. I must say that I have been introduced to some ideas that are new to me, but comfortable. The book, which I read all the way through, was *By Grace Are We Saved*.[3] The title catches our attention because it runs a little against the grain—at least for me. However, I learned that there is more grace in our doctrine than I ever understood before, even if we use a simple definition of grace—as a free gift.

"You may remember from last week's discussion that I

offered the analogy of life and exaltation being like a check-book—I must earn the money in my account, and if I am a little out of balance, grace will make up the difference. Well, I no longer believe that analogy is a good one, though I haven't thought up a better one.

"I now understand," Richard continues, "that Christ's grace begins much earlier than I thought. Further, his grace assists me all along the way. To torture the analogy a little bit, I would say that it is never *my* money in the bank—it is *our* money, his and mine. Then, if I am short, it will be his money alone which balances the account. That's as close as I can come today. Maybe I'll have something better later. By reading Brother Millet's book I think I have an inkling that my understanding of the doctrine of grace has been incomplete at best. I am learning that there is much more to the Atonement than I had ever considered."

Following a short testimony in which Richard expresses his heartfelt appreciation for the Atonement, he sits down.

Brother Thomas, after stating his gratitude for these reports, then calls upon Brother David Bradley, the patriarch.

"I have been richly blessed by being here today. Brother Thomas has asked me to comment on a book by Stephen Robinson titled *Believing Christ*.[4] Brother Robinson has written a very reader-friendly book. His illustrations help make more understandable the complex nature of what Christ did for us. Through this book I am reminded that I don't have to do it all—that it doesn't all depend on me. This is a wonderful book that I would recommend to everyone.

"I also want to add that over the years I have pondered the ideas we have been discussing these past two weeks. My own experiences have led me towards a definition of grace similar to that which Brother Thomas has put on the board. It is clear to me that in many gospel discussions I have participated in, the doctrine of grace has frequently been avoided, as well as misunderstood. In this class, however, I think we are getting closer to a more accurate understanding of this doctrine and how it fits with the Atonement. I thank you, Brother Thomas, for helping us along this lesser-known path of understanding."

With that, Brother Bradley smiles and sits down. Brother Thomas says to the class, "I am sure that there are still unanswered questions within the group today. Some of you may not be satisfied with where we are finishing. With the bishop's permission, I would like to spend one more Sunday on this. As you know, next week is general conference, so it will be in two weeks." The class is then brought to a close.

As authors, we hope you enjoyed attending this Gospel Doctrine class. We have been impressed with your attention— I don't think any of them suspected that we were watching. (Have you ever wondered if there are any watching *us*, unseen but not unconcerned?)

Through this fictional Gospel Doctrine class we have attempted to give you the beginning of a definition of grace. We don't mean to suggest that it is finished. Hopefully it is a place to start. We encourage you to read, reflect, respond, and refine your understanding of the meaning of this vital concept.

Like the members of our imaginary class, we too have enjoyed the books that were reported on. The materials found in these books have forever changed our understanding of the Atonement. There are many other references which might be added, but there is one that must be. This is Elder McConkie's talk "What Think Ye of Salvation by Grace?"[5] which, at least for us, needed to be read more than once.

As the two of us considered how truth is discovered in the gospel, it is clear that our personal experiences add much to enhance our understanding. No one other than Paul himself can truly appreciate his feelings of gratitude for the miracle— the grace of the Lord—demonstrated along the road to Damascus. Neither can any of us fully comprehend the depth of Alma the Younger's feelings of profound humility when he contemplated how close he was to eternal damnation, only to be rescued by the tender mercies of the Master.

It is so with each of us. All the doctrinal discussions and readings of the scriptures that we may do are no substitute for the experiences of our individual lives.

At one time Don wrote to Brent the following: "As I reflect upon my understanding of the principles of the gospel, it is clear that the events of my life have altered that under-standing. While reading, praying, and talking about the Atonement helped me see new ideas, serving others was also vital. However, these everyday experiences seem, in retro-spect, to be groundwork for difficult times. Truly, I cannot overstate the effects that the loss of our son Mitchell has had upon my motivation to more deeply study the Atonement. The events surrounding his passing did more than any other thing to increase the breadth and depth of my sensitivity to and comprehension of the atonement of Jesus Christ!

"All of these happenings—reading the Book of Mormon, studying the words of modern-day prophets and other in-spired brethren, speaking about the Atonement and writing about it, and of course the death of my son—have signifi-cantly altered my life. This, in turn, has made Christ's earthly mission personal to me. Even so, I feel that the door has just been opened to a clearer understanding of the marvelous work of the Savior. I know that there is something here that can sustain me through all of life—that is, through life's ago-nizing pains and difficulties as well as its successes and re-wards.

"The idea expressed in the phrase 'make it more per-sonal' does not do justice to the feelings I have about the Atonement. I truthfully can't tell if I am a late bloomer in dis-covering these ideas about the Atonement, or if I am simply going through a process common to many. Nonetheless, like Ammon, 'I cannot say the smallest part which I feel' " (Alma 26:16).

Like Don, and probably like all of you, I, Brent, have also had numerous experiences in which I can see the hand of the Lord in my life. These experiences have seemingly come at times when I wasn't deserving in any way. Such events have forever changed me and filled me with gratitude for all the Lord did for me in spite of myself.

Now, before we complete this chapter, let us make one other observation. Upon reflection, we wonder how it is that many of us—the rank and file members of the Church—have not found a complete, accurate understanding of the Lord's grace in our lives, while at the same time some of our

Protestant friends seem to appreciate or comprehend some parts of the meaning of grace better than we do. Perhaps it is because we are the workers in the vineyard. We are the laborers in the Lord's kingdom. As such, we laid the foundation, trekked across the plains, then carved out a spiritual base camp in a forsaken desert country. We then built the temples, reared missionaries, and left home and family to preach the gospel while those in other causes seemed to be doing less.

Amid all of this glorious labor and remarkable achievement, perhaps some of us have forgotten or overlooked the fundamental part. While the Brethren have sent a clear signal from Mount Zion, we may have heard only part of that message. Sometimes we have forgotten whose cause this is and in so doing have missed some of the weightier matters.

Have we put our hand to the plow and, in our attempt to avoid looking back, have still not looked ahead? Keeping our eyes down on the work may improve efficiency while decreasing efficacy. If we do not understand that both our performance *and* our reward come by grace, we may lose both enthusiasm and energy. Though the row is long, when we understand that it doesn't depend only on us but that he gives us the power to fulfill our assignments, it is then that we can better withstand the emotional ups and downs of our labors. When we realize that the Savior provides all of this because of his incomprehensible love—and only because of that—the wave of humility that follows this discovery also gives us both true hope and dedication, saturated with stamina.

_____Notes

1. Bruce R. McConkie, "The Purifying Power of Gethsemane," *Ensign*, May 1985, p. 10.
2. See Bruce C. Haften, *The Broken Heart* (Salt Lake City: Deseret Book Co., 1989).

3. See Robert L. Millet, *By Grace Are We Saved* (Salt Lake City: Bookcraft, 1989).

4. Stephen E. Robinson, *Believing Christ* (Salt Lake City: Deseret Book Co., 1992), pp. 30–32. Used by permission.

5. See Bruce R. McConkie, "What Think Ye of Salvation by Grace?" *Brigham Young University 1983–84 Fireside and Devotional Speeches* (Provo, Utah: University Publications, 1984), pp. 44–50.

CHAPTER SIX

When Does His Grace Begin?

Following our fictional Gospel Doctrine class, many members of the group still had unanswered questions. One of those members was Tom Wilson, who had been quite outspoken in both class periods. Since the second Sunday he had been thinking about the discussions and finally decided to call his venerable friend, the stake patriarch, David Bradley.

We suppose that if that conversation actually took place, it might have sounded something like this:

"David, this is Tom Wilson. Do you have a few minutes?"

"For you, of course," David responds warmly. "What's on your mind?"

"I've been thinking quite a bit about our discussion in Sunday School," Tom begins with some hesitation. "I guess I'm troubled about the direction that entire conversation has been going, and I wondered if we might talk about it."

"Certainly," Brother Bradley replies softly. "Would you like me to come over to your home or what?"

"Actually, I'd like to come to your home, if that wouldn't be too much trouble," Tom answers quickly, not wanting to impose anymore than is necessary. "I'll be near there later this afternoon."

"No trouble at all. Would between five and six o'clock be good for you?"

"Perfect. See you then."

As arranged, the two friends get comfortably settled in the Bradley's den a little after five o'clock. The conversation begins with David asking, "Now, Tom, I can tell you're troubled by this, so why don't you try to summarize your concerns."

Immediately feeling at ease, as he knew he would, Tom begins, "My underlying concern, David, has to do with some of the scriptures we discussed in class. I am troubled because several in attendance—you included—seem to have a point of view different from mine. Frankly, prior to these class discussions I have ignored or resisted discussions about grace because I believed that grace only comes into play 'after all we can do.' In other words, I must do my part first, and then grace, whatever it is, happens."

"I see you've taken 2 Nephi 25:23 very literally, haven't you," David says in response.

"Is there any other way to take it?" Tom's voice shows real surprise.

"Let's read it and see." Turning to the verse, he then reads: " 'For we labor diligently to write, to persuade our children, and also our brethren, to believe in Christ, and to be reconciled to God.' " Pausing for a moment, David says, "Tom, almost everyone who discusses this passage ignores the first part that I've just read. If we stress believing in Christ and becoming reconciled to God, it may soften the emphasis on the second part of the passage.

"Now, let me finish it. This is the part that seems to trouble you, isn't it?" Adding a little firmness to his voice, David completes the verse: " 'For we know that it is by grace that we are saved, after all we can do.' "

Tom nods, acknowledging that this, in fact, was the part that was troubling him. David then begins a gentle explanation: "I'll admit that as I have studied the topic of grace, this has been a passage that I have considered intensely. And I think I have some different thoughts and feelings about it than I used to. For a long time I believed that the word *after* in the verse was time related. Simply put, I believed that I had to do all I possibly could do before grace would kick in. I didn't have a clear definition for grace, but I thought it surely must come later, after all my efforts, given the apparent message in that verse. Is that close to how you have felt?"

"Close? It is almost exactly how I feel—right now!" Tom exclaims. "So, what's changed for you, David?"

The patriarch leans back, removes his bifocals, and smiles. "Let me answer your question with a question," he says. "Can you think of experiences in your life where your efforts did not seem to be required before the Lord's tender mercies and grace were given to you?"

"Well, I'm not sure," Tom answers carefully. "I don't think I've ever given that much thought."

"Okay, that's fair. What about answering that question from the point of view of Paul or Alma the Younger, as was talked about in class? Do you suppose that they could think of times in their lives when the tender mercies of the Lord began and they hadn't done all they could do?" David asks the questions gently, wanting not to offend his friend.

"I can see what you're getting at, but I don't know if I buy it. However, if you're right, how do you explain the word *after?*"

"Now, I don't think I necessarily have to explain it," David says carefully. "But I can tell you that over the years I have studied that verse considerably, along with several other references."

"Then give me the benefit of your studies, my friend. It's okay if you just tell me what you think. I have a feeling that you are trying awfully hard to be diplomatic."

"Okay, okay," responds the gentle patriarch, "let me just say that if you read the chapters surrounding 2 Nephi 25, I suspect you'll find that Nephi simply wasn't focusing on the central importance of our works, or 'doing all we can do,' first. In fact, much to the contrary, he was delivering a message concerning the central importance of the mission of the Messiah. Nephi was also trying to help us see the magnitude of the great gifts that come from him.

"For example," he continues, "in 2 Nephi 26 verse 25, Nephi is describing salvation and exaltation when he says, 'Come . . . buy milk and honey, without money and without price.' What does that mean, Tom?"

Tom quickly replies, "Come on, David, both of us are familiar with many scriptures that tell us our works are essential, not just appreciated."

"Truly, Tom, I couldn't agree more; but tonight we're not discussing whether we have obligations as members of the Church of Jesus Christ. Of course we do. Right now, however, we're centering our discussion on the magnitude of the gifts of the Messiah, which are given to those who love him.

"Now," David concludes, "let me ask you another question. Is it possible for me ever to do all I can do?"

"What do you mean?"

"Just exactly what I said. Can you ever actually achieve a point where you have done all you can do?"

"I see what you mean," says Tom. "If we set that standard, then it's impossible to achieve it, right?"

"That's how I see it." David sighs. "If we think we have to complete everything that is possible before his grace can begin, we'll never feel that we've gotten it all done—thus leaving us frustrated and discouraged. I don't think that's the Lord's intent. So the scripture must mean something else, Tom. And that was my conclusion some time ago."

"I can see how you came to that conclusion, but I don't know if I am ready to jump there," Tom replies honestly.

"Fair enough, Tom. Then let me share two other ideas, after which you can think about this conversation for a while and then maybe we can talk again. The first is from the LDS Bible Dictionary, which says, under the topic of 'grace' on page 697: 'It is likewise through the grace of the Lord that individuals, through faith in the atonement of Jesus Christ and repentance of their sins, receive strength and assistance to do good works that they otherwise would not be able to maintain if left to their own means.'

"While this statement is not scripture, Tom, it is wonderfully insightful. The Bible Dictionary goes on to say that this grace is an 'enabling power.' What a very useful idea! To me, this means that grace enables or gives me power to do things I couldn't otherwise do. And it is not necessarily after I have worked my fingers to the bone in trying to do all I can ever possibly do. It can also refer to helping me get started with what I feel a need to do. Sometimes his grace also helps me continue, and sometimes it helps me finish a task when I may have otherwise simply run out of gas."

Tom pauses to read through the Bible Dictionary definition of grace. "I think," he finally says, "that this is a helpful definition. I'll think about it for a few days before I respond to your question—about reaching a point where you've done all you can."

"Sounds good to me," David says encouragingly. "Let's consider a second idea. The words of the prophet Jacob in the Book of Mormon are very helpful in understanding the nature of grace and when it occurs in our lives. In chapter 4 verse 6 of Jacob, we find the following: 'Wherefore, we search the prophets, and we have many revelations and the spirit of prophecy; and having all these witnesses we obtain a hope, and our faith becometh unshaken, insomuch that we truly can command in the name of Jesus and the very trees obey us, or the mountains, or the waves of the sea. Nevertheless, the Lord God showeth us our weakness that we may know that it is by his grace, and his great condescensions unto the children of men, that we have power to do these things.'

"Tom, I will only add this question: If it is by his grace and his 'great condescensions' unto us that we have power to do great works, is it not also by his grace and condescensions that we have power to do *any* good works?"

"That's a fair question," Tom replies with real resolution in his voice. "I'll think about these ideas for a few days. Then maybe we can get together again. Or maybe I'll just respond in the next Gospel Doctrine class, if I'm ready."

"If I know you," David says, smiling, "you'll be ready."

"You know—" Tom pauses and reopens the conversation. "All this discussion has left me with some thoughts about the meaning of the word *after* in the verse we were discussing. It seems that you have avoided giving a direct answer, so that I might try to decide myself. I have been thinking during the conversation tonight that maybe I placed the emphasis incorrectly. For example, if I said, 'It is by grace we are saved, after *all* we can do,' that seems to suggest we can never do enough. Or perhaps 'after all' means 'in spite of.' There's even a possibility that it could be rendered, 'Notwithstanding all we do, we are saved by grace.' What do you think of those ideas?"

"Well, Tom," David cautions, "I have had some of those some thoughts and questions as you have. However, I don't think we need to know a specific answer to appreciate the all-encompassing nature of the Savior's contribution in the eternal future of all of his children—which contribution we may call his grace."

The two friends stand, shake hands, and smile, each appreciating the safety felt in the conversation, and each continuing to ponder David's final question. It is a fitting place to conclude their conversation.

Our goal in sharing this conversation was to introduce you to or reemphasize the importance of considering a broader interpretation of 2 Nephi 25:23. We have decided to conclude this chapter with an experience that happened to Don—an experience that stretches out over the past thirty-five years.

This story may be another example of serendipity, or maybe I (Don) am just a slow learner. In the wonderful work *Les Misérables*, the concept of grace is the central but unspoken theme. When I was in the ninth grade, I read Victor Hugo's remarkable book for an English class assignment. It was a startling experience. I was fascinated by the ability of the author to create such vivid images with words. Equally impressive was the powerful effect the story and the interaction of the characters had upon my emotions.

In reading this book, I ached for and wept with Jean Valjean, the main character, and otherwise vicariously experienced the extreme and difficult vicissitudes in his life. Many of those thoughts and feelings that were embedded in my fourteen-year-old mind remain with me to this day.

Years later I went to see the musical version of the book as it played on Broadway. Actually, I saw it twice. As I watched the struggles and triumphs of the characters on stage, I had feelings similar to those I had experienced many years earlier. Most important to me was the experience I had the second time I attended the musical. By this time I had been through most of the experiences that led to our writing this book. Indeed, I had a different perspective.

During the play, I saw visually an illustration of the relationship between grace and works as it played out in the life of Jean Valjean. In his early years, and somewhat innocently, he stole a loaf of bread in an attempt to provide food for his sister and her seven young children. For this outrageous crime he was imprisoned for nineteen years. Originally the sentence was only five years, but it was lengthened because of his numerous attempts to escape. Eventually Valjean served out his time and was released.

But Valjean's struggles were far from over. His status as a felon led to cruel and unjust treatment wherever he went, and his anger and vengefulness continued to grow.

Turned away from every inn, tavern, and residence he visited, Valjean finally found himself at the home of a Catholic bishop, Monseigneur Bienvenu, a kindly man who willingly took him in. That night, however, Valjean's angry, irrational passion took over. He forgot the kindness extended to him and remembered only the injustices of his imprisonment; and his desire for revenge against any and all led him to steal the bishop's valuable silver plates. As he made his escape over the garden wall, he drew the attention of the local police officers, who took him into custody. Upon discovering the silver in Valjean's knapsack, they accused him of stealing, though Valjean claimed the plates were a gift. The officers immediately took him back to the scene of his crime to face the bishop.

To Valjean's amazement, the bishop not only corroborated his story but asked why he had not taken the candlestick holders, as had been offered. The officers were surprised but satisfied. The response of the bishop saved Valjean from returning to his life of incarceration. This act of grace also gave him the financial means to start his life anew. A covenant was then made as the repentant thief promised to remember that God who saved him.

From the simple act of the bishop, the transformation of Jean Valjean began. In a short time his heart changed forever. Throughout the rest of his life, Valjean's own personal grace and majesty grew to exceed that of the acts that transformed *him*. Surely he would never say that he was saved by works! Not even the tenderness of heart within him was of his own making. From that day of reclamation forward, Jean Valjean's behavior reflected that simple act of grace.

During the second time I watched the musical, I gained a wonderful insight. It had to do with the timing of grace in Valjean's life. Grace began well before any of his efforts. His life was changed by grace, and then his behavior began to reflect the effects of the charitable acts of the priest.

Is this not so with us? King Benjamin called us unprofitable servants, and it is true. We really can't even take credit for our acts of grace, our so-called good works. The power to do them—to perform good works—also comes from the Savior.

We don't know exactly how this process works; we just know that it does. We can feel how it works, however. And it feels as though his grace has always been there. His grace gives us power that enables us to perform acts of grace, which gradually transform us as we become more and more like him.

CHAPTER SEVEN

A Broken Heart:
Grace from the Inside Out

In the lives of men and women there is occasionally a confluence of events that, while they have no demonstrable direct relationship, cannot be simply circumstantial. Such is the case with all that is described in this chapter. Because of the nature of these events, we proceed cautiously, not wanting to offend anyone with this discussion.

Don shares the following experience:

Mitchell had a tenacity unlike that of any of our other children. Fearless in the face of opposition, he taught us many lessons. An early result of my contact with his tenacious spirit taught me a lesson from which I hopefully will never recover.

One evening when Mitch was about four or five years old, my wife, Diane, had left me home to watch the kids while she was shopping. It was getting late and I had put all the kids to bed—several times each, I might add. As is the case in many homes, in our home at bedtime one or two of the children resisted the gentle entreaties of their parents to "please go along to bed." To add complexity to the problem, it seemed that the torch of bedtime resistance was passed around from child to child, depending on the night or circumstance. On this particular night it was, so it seemed, Mitch's turn, and he carried out his resistance in characteristic fashion. Relentless, fearless even, he came back time after time trying to renegotiate a later bedtime hour.

"Thirty minutes more, Dad, please?"

"Please, son, go on up to bed."

He went back up to his bedroom. A short time passed.

"What if I keep my room cleaner all week?"

"I don't think so. It's late and I'm busy, so just go to bed."

I could hear his footsteps going slowly back up the stairs. A few more minutes passed. Silently and without my knowing, he crept down the stairs from his bedroom while I sat quietly at the kitchen table preparing materials for our stake conference the next day. We were having a special General Authority visitor, I was counselor to the stake president, and I felt some pressure to do my part well. I no sooner got back to my work, when there he was, standing in the doorway to the kitchen.

"Dad?"

"What?" I responded impatiently.

"If I never ask to stay up again, can I just this once?"

"No, Mitch. N-O, no!" I said, spelling the letters out. "Can you understand *no?* No! Now, march back up those stairs and don't come back down!"

Quietly, he turned around, then ran up the stairs. I turned again to my papers, trying to get back into the spirit of preparation. I had been writing for only a few minutes when again I heard from the kitchen doorway, "Dad?"

Incredulous, and with extreme frustration, I responded in a loud voice, "*What?*"

I turned to see his tear-stained face mouth these words in a near whisper, "Do you love me?"

That night a lesson was learned with a child as the teacher. The most important question was asked, and then hopefully answered as I invited him over to sit in my lap and talk awhile. He raced across the room and jumped into my arms. In a few minutes and after a drink of water and so on, he went back to bed—this time for good—and I returned to my preparation for the next two day's conference sessions.

In the early afternoon of the following day, I drove over to the stake center. It was in the spring of 1979. I had been recently called as counselor, and our first stake conference visitor was Elder Marion D. Hanks. The stake presidency, clerks, and executive secretaries were gathered in the stake offices waiting for Elder Hanks's arrival. Because this was our first General Authority visitor, we were anxious that everything go just right.

Elder Hanks arrived by car, traveling alone, and as we watched him walk up the sidewalk our collective nervousness continued to increase. We were anxiously gathered around the big glass door entryway, which he came through as he entered the stake offices. I guess he could feel our anxiety. His gentle comment was unforgettable to me. He looked at each of us and then said, "Brethren, you look a little nervous, but you have nothing to worry about. It's just me. So relax; we're going to have a wonderful time." The tension immediately left, and thus began an unforgettable experience.

Later that evening, during the last session of the day, Elder Hanks looked out at the gathering of stake members and commented that he wanted to talk with us about something that he rarely discussed. He expressed positive feelings about the group in attendance, saying that he felt an unusual spirit among us, which would allow him to speak openly about a difficult subject. He addressed the subject of suicide and gave comforting words to any who had suffered pain because a loved one or close associate had taken his or her own life.

I left the meeting a little puzzled. I had heard things I had never before considered, and I frankly wondered about their usefulness.

Within a few days after the stake conference, my home teaching companion, an eighteen-year-old priest, apparently took his own life. I spoke at the funeral, having been guided by the words of Elder Hanks. It was a difficult assignment, and I wondered if anything I said had value for the family or the congregation.

Many years passed without another reason to consider this perplexing topic. In fact, it was almost exactly thirteen years later, in the spring of 1992, when I learned that a couple who were good friends of mine had lost a son in circumstances tragically similar to that of my previous home teaching companion. This seventeen-year-old youth took his own life in a moment of deep discouragement. I felt overwhelmed with compassion for this family, and I immediately wrote their name on my "to do" list, intending to call them that same day.

The day passed quickly; I wasn't sure what to say, so I rescheduled the call to another day. After two or three weeks of postponing the call, I confronted myself directly, saying, *Don, even if it is uncomfortable, you need to either make the call or quit writing it on your list of things to do.* Appropriately chastised, I decided to make the call.

As I thought about what I might say, I remembered the thoughtful address of Elder Hanks those many years earlier. I wondered if he might have time to talk to the family, and so, after giving the idea a little thought, I picked up the telephone, called the Church office building information number, and asked for Elder Hanks.

When I reached Elder Hanks's secretary, she asked me if he was expecting a call from me. I told her that he was not and that I wasn't really anyone important, but that I just needed to talk with him for a few minutes. She then reminded me that it was 5:30 P.M. She wasn't resisting me, she said, but just wondered if he would even be in his office. I hadn't realized the lateness of the hour; it was two hours later on the East coast, where I was, but I hadn't looked at my watch before making the call.

Without further discussion, she agreed to ring his office number. In a moment, Elder Hanks's familiar deep voice came on the line. I reintroduced myself to him, reminding him of the talk he had given so many years earlier. I asked him if he had a few moments to talk with me about a problem. His response reduced all my anxiety about having made the call.

"Don," he said gently, "I don't have anything to do until a little after six, so we have all the time we need."

I then proceeded to tell him of my friends' recent tragedy, and asked if he would have time to speak with them. He was encouraging, and excused himself from the line for a moment to check his schedule. When he returned, he spoke again in the gentle language of one dedicated to serving others. Enthusiastically he said, "Don, we're in luck. After my 6:30 meeting, I don't have anywhere to go, so I'll be home all evening. If they want, they can call me at home this evening after 7:30."

Immediately after the close of our conversation, I called my friends, and the wife answered. I expressed my sorrow and sympathy for the tragic and difficult loss of her son. Additionally, I attempted to comfort her by telling her the confidence I had in her as a mother and that she shouldn't draw inappropriate conclusions from this event. Finally, we talked about my conversation with Elder Hanks, and I gave her his phone number. Our conversation ended, and I felt re-assured that Elder Hanks would help them find some semblance of peace in their loss, if they would only call him.

A few weeks passed, and I found myself wondering if they had placed the call to Elder Hanks. Even though I thought of them several times, I somehow couldn't bring my-self to call them. I just couldn't think of a good reason to in-quire. I didn't want them to think I was pressuring them if they hadn't made the call. Nor did I want them to think I was looking for a pat on the back if they had. So I just let it go. It was, only a short time, however, before I found out the an-swer to my question.

It seems appropriate for Brent to describe some events which took place only six months later:

Three years ago, early on a Sunday morning in the fall of 1992, I (Brent) received a most distressing call from Don in New England. I had never heard his voice sound like it then did. In a hushed voice, he said to me, "Brent, I need help . . . I need your help. We have lost Mitchell. He has passed away, he . . . he has taken his own life and I need your help."

"Oh, Don," I gasped, "how can I help you? What can I do?" I desperately wanted to be with him in Massachusetts, rather than two thousand miles away in Utah. "I'll do any-thing I can."

"I'm not sure," Don replied in a coarse whisper. "We just found out late last night, and I can't even begin to understand it. I just needed to talk to someone outside the family who wouldn't criticize Mitch. So after notifying my family members, who were, of course, supportive, I called you.

"Suicide, Brent . . . *suicide!* What has he *done?* I know you loved Mitch, so I knew we could talk a little about this. I also needed someone to contact our friends in Utah, and I wondered if you would do that for me."

For a few minutes we talked of the many wonderful people who were mutually good friends. We talked about our associates in the Church Educational System and our dear friends in the Granite Stake in Sandy, where we had both lived for several years. This distracted Don briefly, and then he continued.

"Brent, could you come out here and speak at his funeral? I know how much you loved Mitch, and how close you felt to him."

It was true. Mitch might well have been my favorite among the six Mangum boys. They're all good boys, but Mitch and I had a closer relationship. I had been his bishop and his friend. In short, I knew Mitch from the inside out.

I agreed to come out and do whatever I could. Don and I spoke for some time about Mitch's emotional state at the time of his death. I could feel Don's anguish but of course could not begin to comprehend it. I just wanted to be there and try to assuage some of the pain that he and his wife, Diane, and their other children were experiencing.

To complete the story, I asked Don if he would include in this chapter some comments from his journal. Reluctant, at first because of a desire to maintain privacy, Don agreed. He wrote:

> Diane and I learned of Mitchell's death late one Saturday evening. We were returning home from a charity event for the Boy Scouts of America. As we drove into the driveway, we could see our bishop's car parked at the end of the drive. The car was empty, it was almost midnight, and something was wrong . . .
>
> Filled with anxiety, I ran ahead to the front door. I could see each tile on the sidewalk—I seemed to be walking in slow

motion—but only seconds had passed when I reached the door. It was locked, so I rang my own doorbell. The door opened and there stood our bishop, face drawn and sober.

"Please go and get Diane," he said very gently.

"What's wrong, Bishop?" I asked in a pleading voice.

"Please go and get your wife," was his only response.

Quickly I turned and ran down the sidewalk toward the driveway. Diane was just getting out of the car, so I put my arm gently around her shoulders and we returned anxiously to the house.

"Bishop, what has happened?" we both asked, not wanting to hear the answer.

"You've lost Mitch," he said, reaching out to catch us as we both collapsed in his arms.

"Bishop, how did this happen?" we pleaded, hoping for a reasonable answer which would help make this somehow sensible.

Because he did not know the details, the bishop deferred, saying that we would be getting a phone call that would give us all more information.

Not wanting to wait, I then asked one of the most difficult questions of my life. "Bishop, did he do this to himself?"

Reluctantly he answered, "Yes." We sobbed uncontrollably as he shared additional details of Mitch's death and as we waited for the phone call from Provo, Utah, where Mitch had been attending Brigham Young University.

Within a few moments the call from Provo came. It was our oldest son, Donald, who was also attending BYU. He told us additional details of Mitch's death. When we finished that difficult discussion, we made provisions for Donald's quick return home later that day.

During the next several hours, from midnight to about 4:00 A.M., a whirlwind of events followed. Our son Marc and daughter-in-law Jenn arrived, along with our home teacher and his wife, who were, coincidentally, also Marc's in-laws. Marc and Jenn had been staying in their home, about half an hour away from us, while Marc, a recent BYU graduate, sought employment in the Boston area. As they came into the house, cautious and gentle words of comfort passed among all of us.

Marc and Jenn brought with them their infant son, David, who was only five weeks old. David, of course, was unaware of all that was happening, but he stayed awake and was very responsive. He was a wonderful source of physical comfort to me, as I frequently held him tightly in my arms and reflected on the child gone and the infant who just recently arrived from the presence of Heavenly Father.

During those early morning hours we also made arrangements for those unbelievable, seemingly unnatural events which must follow a death. The discussions about transporting his body back to Massachusetts and about the funeral and the burial seemed as though they must be happening to another family. We wondered if we were living someone else's life. But we weren't, and the events pressed forward, even though we didn't want to face any of them.

Sometime that morning, Marc told me about a comment he had made in the car while traveling to our house. Reflecting on the cause of Mitchell's death, he had told the others, "This will come as no surprise to my parents—a shock, of course, but no surprise." While not knowing of the real difficulty which Mitchell had faced, he was aware that there were problems because of special family fasts and priesthood blessings given to Mitch.

When Marc told me this, his comment opened a floodgate of memories about Mitchell—beginning with the memory of our discovery two years earlier of Mitchell's severe depression, with which he had struggled for many years. These struggles had led to two previous attempts at suicide, both within the previous three years. Through the help of a school counselor, Mitch came home one day and told us of these attempts and of his depression. It is probably true that he was finally at an age where he could articulate his feelings, face his pain, and seek help. Following the revelation of his despondency, we sought help through a professional therapist. In addition, Mitch chose to talk about his circumstances with only one friend. He did not want others to be aware of his challenges and treat him differently, so he did not discuss these matters with anyone else. We, of course, honored his desires.

So while Marc had not been fully aware of Mitchell's condition, he was certain that we knew that Mitch was high risk. These memories and thoughts filled my mind while we worked through the arrangements during those early Sunday morning hours.

I thought of the afternoon the previous June when we had taken Mitch to the airport to send him off to summer school at BYU. As Diane and I returned to the car after saying our good-byes to him, I told Diane, "I know that we need to give him the opportunity to go, but I just hope he returns home." Sadly, he did not.

All these statements about depression and despondency do not truly capture the essence of a wonderful son with a difficult problem. Because no one knew of his depression except those mentioned, he was able to be his normal, outgoing self most of the time. The professional who assisted him taught him that he felt a wider range of emotions than most others. His highs were higher and his lows were lower. He faced his lows privately with no support outside of his parents and the therapist.

His deeply felt emotions provided him with some wonderful traits. He had a tender heart for the lonely and isolated. While some might reasonably expect a child to buckle and withdraw to his room under the staggering load of the type of depression Mitch faced, such was not the case with him. In fact, Mitch frequently found relief from his suffering by turning outward. Service to others, not to self, gave him strength to continue and move forward during times when he otherwise would have been immobilized from feelings of deep discouragement. It was his pattern to not withdraw from others when these bouts of depression would occur. He had learned from the therapist to get out with others when these feelings would take hold of him.

During the first hours after receiving the news, I recalled a typical event the previous summer when I had tried to help him. I was then serving as stake Young Men's president, and Mitch was on the stake youth committee. We were attending youth conference together. On this particular evening, while the youth were involved in a dance, I was in a classroom, interviewing candidates for the next year's youth committee. While in such an interview, Mitch broke into the room and announced that he really needed to talk with me. I could tell he was agitated, so I excused myself and we walked together to another room.

"What's the matter, son?" I asked gently.

"It's coming, Dad, it's coming! How do I stop it?" He was speaking of an overwhelming feeling of darkness, loneliness, and pain—a feeling I could not fully comprehend. I just felt it a privilege to try to help him resist.

"Do you know what is driving it?" I asked, really trying to help us both understand a little better.

"Well," Mitch replied nervously, "I was sitting in the cultural hall with a boy who is new in the stake. In getting acquainted with him, I could tell that he was very sad, and so I asked him why. After visiting for a while, the boy told me of the severe abuse he had suffered at the hands of his father. I tried to encourage him, and he seemed to cheer up. However, as he described this abuse in some detail, that's when the darkness began . . ."

Somehow I understood that Mitch had internalized the other boy's pain. We talked about this for some time, and gradually the pain and darkness seemed to dissipate and Mitch was able to go back into the dance with a cheerful heart. I felt privileged to help him through this difficulty. He was such a good and caring boy. If only he could get these feelings of depression out of his system. Those were my thoughts that night as Mitch told me about his experience. I reflected on the moments of that summer evening several times during the early morning hours after we found out about Mitchell's death.

After several anguish-filled hours, Diane and I tried to rest, but sleep would not come. Our bodies would shut down from sheer exhaustion for short periods of time, and then we would again awaken to go through the seemingly endless cycle of questions.

The second evening, in the very early morning hours, I awoke—again from a fitful sleep. Diane was finally sleeping, so I lay there quietly, sorting through a myriad of disjointed thoughts. After a few moments, I noticed that the room was filled with a tangible quietness. I said silently into the darkness, *Where is my son? Is he safe? Is he warm? Does he need a blanket? Is Heavenly Father mad at him? Please, oh please, can I find these answers? I must have answers and not just someone else's stories.* Silence sometimes brings serenity. The room was still.

The next day, Monday, there was an outpouring of love and concern from all corners of our lives. None of it was wasted. About 4:30 that afternoon, the phone rang and someone came up to my room to tell me that Elder Marion D. Hanks was on the phone. I had to admit that I had thought of him all day but could not find within myself the power to call him.

I picked up the phone and heard his familiar voice as he asked how I was doing. He told me that three people had called him early that morning to tell him of our grief, and that he was honored to be included in assisting. Further, he said that he had waited until late to call because he had spent the day considering what he might say to us. Truly, the call itself was enough, but his encouraging words had true healing power.

I asked Elder Hanks if he had heard from my friends who had lost their son the previous spring. He told me that he had had a lovely visit with them. He then spoke of the irony that related my current situation to the call I had made for my friends.

He asked how Diane was doing and suggested that we get her on the phone, which I did. For the next forty-five minutes he taught us how to deal with the feelings of pain and sorrow we were experiencing. We took careful notes to review when our clouds of grief cleared.

The conversation was over all too soon. Little echoes still surround Diane and me even now, three years later. We also had many other helpful calls from close friends and associates that eased the burden.

I have been reluctant to share the story of Mitchell's death because of its overwhelming personal nature, and so I have tried to be both brief and discreet. With the loss of our son, our grief was immediate, overwhelming, and nearly palpable. With the help of others, the pain was eased. Though we knew that Mitchell would never again walk down the stairs and ask if he could stay up a little later, and that he had "gone upstairs" for the last time, as time passed we found peace and consolation in the knowledge of the love and mercy of Christ. Now, three years later, we have hope in the glorious resurrection and feel secure in the fact that Mitch is tucked safely in the blankets of love provided by the Savior.

We have titled this chapter "A Broken Heart: Grace from the Inside Out." All discussions about grace may be only academic until one experiences the need for the Lord's grace. As we have continued to study the Atonement through reading the Book of Mormon, we have learned that for the Mangum family, it was no longer academic. Most of us are unable to understand the Lord's grace until we truly see it in action and feel it in our lives.

Who else can really understand the pain of a personal loss or a difficult circumstance other than those directly involved? Perhaps only those who have experienced a similar loss can comprehend it. Even so, not even they can give total comfort. That comes solely from the One who has an infinite capacity to feel the pains of his people. His suffering was so great that he understands all pain and all suffering.

The admonition of the Master "And ye shall offer for a sacrifice unto me a broken heart and a contrite spirit" (3 Nephi 9:20) has new meaning to those who have suffered such pain. The comfort given is always greater than the pain.

This comfort provides a new relationship between the distressed and the Comforter. When a heart is broken and the Healer intervenes, the relationship between the two is forever changed; for in the midst of their mini-Gethsemane, the sorrowing find solace in the *real* Gethsemane. Christ truly descended below all things. Most important, in our times of isolation we find consolation from him who knows what it means to be left alone.

Such grief and pain may be required of most of us. Elder Neal A. Maxwell taught us that "if our hearts are set too much upon the things of this world, they must be broken."[1] A broken heart can come when we acknowledge our inability to do all that is expected, recognize our sins, suffer grief, experience a difficult circumstance, or feel discouragement. If our extremity is God's opportunity, his response is only to bless those in severe circumstances. In such conditions come remarkable moments of discovering the meaning of grace and the effectiveness of the Atonement.

_____NOTES

1. Neal A. Maxwell, *Notwithstanding My Weakness* (Salt Lake City: Deseret Book Co., 1981), pp. 66–67.

CHAPTER EIGHT

The Condescension of God: Seeing the Lord's Mercy in His Handiwork

Trials and tragedies may lead us to Christ and result in dynamic changes within us, but only if we choose to let them. We must also choose to surrender to the Savior. As Dietrich Bonhoeffer stated, "When Christ calls a man, he bids him come and die."[1] The possibility of our surrendering to the Savior is frequently enhanced by our seeing how he has condescended to help us. He has condescended to us in many ways, some of which we will now consider.

To do this, let us return to the East Coast and visit another fictional institute class taught by Brother Terrance Matthews. This particular class is actually a special monthly symposium created to appeal to students of science. Brother Matthews holds nine of these during the school year and, with the help of some student advisers, selects gospel topics often tied to scientific themes for each presentation.

Brother Matthews is particularly well equipped to deal with some of these topics, as he holds an undergraduate degree in physics. He has also maintained more than just a passing interest in current issues related to cosmology or the origin of the universe. His self-deprecating humor tends to understate his awareness of the physical sciences. In the past some students initially underestimated his background, but sooner or later they grew to appreciate his ability to help them resolve seeming paradoxes between science and the gospel.

Tonight is the first class of the new semester, and there are a lot of new faces present. In all, thirty-two students have shown up for the course. From previous years' experience, Brother Matthews knows that tonight's audience will be a rich mixture of young people of deep gospel conviction, as well as some who are struggling with their faith. He also knows that he cannot completely resolve the concerns of some of his students; he just wants to give them some ammunition to be used when necessary.

Brother Matthews spent much of the previous summer in Utah, although in late August he did travel up to Vancouver, British Columbia, to be with his brother and sister-in-law. On the trip back to Salt Lake he had an unusual encounter, which has continued to replay in his mind. He knows that he will start the class by talking about his trip. As further preparation for this evening, he previously visited extensively with his student advisory committee and asked them to be prepared to participate in the discussion.

After some brief introductory remarks, Brother Matthews begins by introducing himself in his characteristically self-effacing style. "I must admit," he begins, "that I am an amateur cosmologist—one who studies the cosmos and the origin of the universe. I marvel at the complexity of the Lord's creations, some of which we can see when we look out away from the earth into the night sky. The order found in the Lord's creations, along with the obvious attention given the most minute of details, adds to my sense of humility. When I consider the majesties of Heavenly Father's creations, I am overwhelmed by his love and caring for us, his children. I believe, like Alma, that 'all things denote there is a God; yea, even the earth, and all things that are upon the face of it, yea, and its motion, yea, and also all the planets which move in their regular form do witness that there is a Supreme Creator.' (Alma 30:44.)

"Because I enjoy reading popular-science books," Brother Matthews continues, "I have, as you might expect, studied

Stephen Hawking's book *A Brief History of Time.*[2] When the movie of the same name was released, my wife, Kate, and I went to it, although she didn't particularly enjoy it. I did, however, and was appreciative that she allowed me to indulge myself.

"Thinking that the world was like me and that this would be a very popular movie, I convinced Kate that we should arrive at the theater early. Talking her into going at all was the real sales job, so convincing her to go early was relatively easy.

"Anyway, we arrived at the theater about a half hour in advance of the starting time. I rushed to the box office to see if we were going to have trouble getting in. The young woman selling tickets looked at me strangely when I asked her if there were tickets left. She responded affirmatively, and I was relieved. As it turned out, we were the first people in the theater. A few minutes later a small cluster of people— maybe ten or fifteen—joined us. They sat together in the back, and we were the only people to watch the movie."

Brother Matthews can tell that his class is caught up in his introductory story, and so he proceeds, adding energy to his voice.

"As the film went on, I discovered that the other people attending were not 'amateur cosmologists.' During sections of the film when I was really straining to understand the technical discussion, they would laugh heartily. I didn't laugh at those parts, simply because I didn't 'get it.' I have since wondered if they 'got it' or if they had simply been assigned by university professors to attend and weren't even paying attention. In truth, Kate barely stayed awake, except during the biographical portions of the film.

"Like so many amateur cosmologists," he continues, "I have devoured Hawking's writings, and when he traveled to the New England area, I attended his lectures. I just find learning about the mysteries and grandeur of the Lord's creations to be tremendously fascinating. Beyond that, I am profoundly humbled at the majesty of our Heavenly Father's works, both visible and invisible.

"With this introduction, let's get into this evening's discussion, which I have chosen to call 'Science and the Condescension of God: Seeing the Lord's Mercy in His Handiwork.' Could someone give us a working definition of *condescend* or *condescension?*"

A hand comes up, and Brother Matthews acknowledges it with a nod. The student desiring to respond is Thomas McKenzie from Texas. He states, "Well, Brother Matthews, I believe that to condescend, in the way you're intending, means to go down from a higher level to a lower one."

"Thanks, Tom," says Brother Matthews. "That gets us off to a good start. Will someone please read our focus passage for tonight—1 Nephi 11:16–17?"

Alison Merrill from Carlsbad, Kentucky, and a graduate student in astronomy, volunteers. Brother Matthews nods but then says, "The first verse is a question asked of Nephi by a heavenly visitor. And, Alison, as you read the reference, please pause between verses."

Sister Merrill begins. "Let's see, the first verse says, 'And he [the angel] said unto me: Knowest thou the condescension of God?' That seems pretty short for an entire verse."

"It is short," Brother Matthews replies, "so let's look at the whole chapter for a minute. Brothers and sisters, what was happening here, and why did the angel ask this question?"

Some of the students from the advisory committee knew what the subject would be and fortunately have read the assigned passages. When no one else raises a hand, Bob Sparks, a member of the committee, says, "Well, Nephi wanted to know details about his father's vision of the tree of life. This chapter is the Lord's response to Nephi's inquiry. It seems that the question asked by the angel was the Lord's method to set Nephi up for the remarkable visions that followed."

"It sounds to me like someone has been reading the lesson plan," Alison quickly asserts.

"No doubt," Brother Matthews agrees. "Now, let's look at Nephi's response to the question of whether or not he understood God's condescension. Please read the next verse, Alison."

"It says, 'And I said unto him: I know that he loveth his children; nevertheless, I do not know the meaning of all things.'"

Brother Matthews, obviously impressed with the passage, declares, "I love Nephi's response, partly because of the setting—in the midst of a frank and open discussion with a heavenly messenger. This passage is also a favorite of mine because Nephi's words are indicative of his humility. I guess you couldn't bluff an angel anyway. Now, are there any other observations about this passage?"

Mary McDaniel, who just returned from a mission in Spain and is an undergraduate student in biochemistry, raises her hand and says, "I particularly like the rest of the chapter. As you know, what happens in the verses that follow involves a wonderful vision in which Nephi sees the condescension of God. Are we going to discuss that?"

"Yes we are," Brother Matthews replies. "But before we get into that, I want to describe a trip I made this summer. As several of you know, I spent some time out in Salt Lake City, vacationing with my family and also attending classes for institute teachers. During a break in these classes, Kate and I drove our family up to Vancouver to be with my brother, Bill, his wife, Karen, and their children.

"After several days of sight-seeing with them, Kate and the kids left early so that she could meet her sister in Salt Lake, who was driving up from Los Angeles to see her. The children were anxious to get back to Salt Lake and play with their California cousins. I stayed behind to spend a little more time with my brother and, if possible, play a little golf with him. We did this, of course, for our intellectual growth," he inserts, looking for audience response.

After an audible moan from the group, which lets Brother Matthews know they were paying attention, he continues. "Anyway, I flew back to Salt Lake several days later. It is a little difficult to get into Utah from Vancouver using my preferred airline company, since there aren't any direct routes. So I ended up going through Portland, Oregon, where I changed planes.

"It was lunchtime when I arrived at the terminal, and I tried to find a place to eat before my plane took off. As you know, airline food is not always provided on short hops, but as luck would have it, right there in the terminal was a Wendy's, my favorite fast-food establishment. After getting my order, I began looking for a place to sit. The restaurant was totally crowded, and there were no vacant tables. A young lady noticed my dilemma, however, and graciously offered me a place to sit by her. I gratefully accepted, and after introductions, we began to get acquainted.

"This young lady said that her name was Laura, that she was from a nearby community and was going to Utah on the same flight as mine. As we ate, Laura told me that she had left her home in Ohio sometime after high school and had gone to Utah to be with a girlfriend. Eventually she ended up at Weber State University in Ogden, Utah, where she studied in the biological science field. She indicated that she eventually married a young man from Ogden and had ended up moving to Medford, Oregon.

"I dropped several hints about my affiliations with the Church without speaking of it directly. For example, I told her that I had interrupted my education at Boston University for two years and had met my wife while on a subsequent visit to Utah. However, she didn't pick up on any of my hints or in any way ask about the Church. So, feeling unusually constrained, I left it alone.

"In a short time I finished my meal, then excused myself. As I mentioned, we were going to be on the same plane, but I wanted to board early. So I left Laura's table, thanking her for her kindness in offering me a place to sit. I immediately boarded the plane and became comfortably seated. I was assigned an aisle seat on a side row, which I prefer. The window seat next to me wasn't occupied.

"I had just settled in when I felt a tap on my shoulder. It was Laura, and she asked me if I would like company. Normally I would resist such an offer because of the appearance of things, but this young lady was young enough to be my daughter, and I probably looked the age of Noah to her.

Further, I could tell she wanted to talk. I thus invited her to sit down, but before we could even start talking, the passenger assigned to the seat taken by Laura arrived and indicated that this was his spot. I was somewhat surprised that Laura then negotiated a seat exchange with the other passenger. As she did, it was obvious that she really had something on her mind.

"Notwithstanding Laura's apparent urgency, she began very slowly. She first asked me about the tremors she had noticed in my hands while we were eating. These tremors, I explained, were genetic in origin and provided me with no disability that I know of. My mother, I added, and some of my cousins possessed the same trait. Laura indicated that she had an occupational disability with her own hands. It was some kind of arthritis which left her unable to perform many normal functions. In a very compassionate way, she asked if my fingers were painful, as hers were. I told her no.

"I replied that the only time I really felt uncomfortable was when partaking of the sacrament while sitting on the stand. This was because I thought others could see my hands shake a little, and I wondered if that made me somehow appear nervous. I felt that by including a church reference I could open up a discussion about the gospel. So I told her a little about the sacrament and why I, now serving as a bishop out here in Massachusetts, would be sitting in front of the congregation. After that quick explanation, I asked Laura if she was familiar with the sacrament as used in The Church of Jesus Christ of Latter-day Saints.

"She immediately indicated that she had been a member of 'that church' but wasn't any longer. When I asked her some of the details, she told me that she had converted to Mormonism when she came west. But after many years of belonging, she just slipped into inactivity.

"I asked what happened to her that caused her to take this route, and she explained that the years immediately following her baptism were happy ones. The influence of the Church was positive, and the people made her feel comfortable. However, as she got into upper division science courses, she began to have discomfort. She felt that she saw significant conflict between Church doctrine and a variety of scientific issues. She used evolution, the 'big bang' theory, and no demonstrable presence of God in history as examples of the problems she felt she couldn't explain. Then she indicated that with these problems churning in her mind, she had just gradually drifted away.

"As the conversation moved along, I asked Laura why she had approached me in the plane. She told me that she wasn't exactly sure. She indicated that there were several reasons, she supposed. At first she was curious about my shaky hands because of the problems she was having with arthritis. She was also very intrigued with the fact that, though she could tell that I was a Mormon, I hadn't pushed it on her. And finally, she indicated that there was also just something about our conversation that made her want to talk further.

"After Laura answered my question, I inquired about some of the underlying issues that had caused her inactivity and subsequent withdrawal from the Church. In response to the issues she raised, we talked about the apparent evidences of a divine Creator and about the faith in God that many scientists possess. She acknowledged that she was aware of such men and women, but it didn't do much for her. Further, we talked about her tender feelings in the early years after her conversion and gave a name to the source of those many sweet promptings. I helped her understand that she had been feeling the Spirit of the Lord.

"Laura listened intently and asked very forthright and demanding questions. I cannot say to you that I answered everything to her satisfaction, because I didn't. Even so, I can say that the peace that comes when the Spirit is present was felt by both of us.

"Even though the issues remained largely unresolved, I felt like our conversation was meaningful to Laura. As is frequently the case in discussions such as these, only time will determine whether she will allow the Spirit back into her life.

"Now, class," Brother Matthew concludes, "during the days that immediately followed the flight from Portland, I once again thought about the many questions that come from some students of the sciences, like Laura. I also considered the group that I knew would be gathered here tonight, and I looked forward to discussing some of my thoughts with you.

"It is clear to me, and has been for a long time, that scientists with faith find evidence of God in their work. Latter-day Saint scientists find remarkable things to share with us that build our faith. Their perspective adds much to our feelings about the grace of God. When we look at the wonders of the universe and think about the Creator, it is easy to feel that he gives marvelous gifts to us. These are truly gifts, and we have no apparent right to them, other than his good will."

At this point, Brother Matthews tells the class that it is time for a break. The class is two hours in length, and he knows that timely breaks make for good attention. For our readers, we might suggest a little break as well, but don't consume a lot of calories, and don't be gone too long.

After about fifteen minutes, the institute class resumes. Brother Matthews continues by saying, "I have asked Anne Forrestal, a senior at MIT studying astrophysics, to give us a little report."

Anne, a gregarious personality and one who is loved by all who know her, stands up and begins to share her thoughts about God's creations. Although she has notes in her hands, she glances at them only occasionally. By nature an enthusiastic person, she immediately draws everyone in with her warmth.

"There is nothing I would rather do than bear my testimony by talking about my studies. Some of my associates at school may get a little tired of my otherworldly observations, but most of them find them interesting.

"Let me give you an example." Anne is racing through her sentences, and everyone is listening intently, partially because they have to in order to keep up with her.

"Do you know," she continues, "that George Smoot, a former MIT student and now an internationally known cosmologist, discovered 'wrinkles in time'? Of course you don't, unless you follow this stuff. Well, 'wrinkles in time' are a little more than Brother Matthews wanted us to consider, so we won't; but I do want to tell you one thing that Smoot said."

Anne's rat-a-tat manner of speaking is engaging, and the class is spellbound. "Following his momentous discovery," she continues, "which, by the way, Stephen Hawking called the scientific discovery of the century, if not all time, Smoot wrote a book. It has been appropriately titled *Wrinkles in Time*.

"In his book Smoot made this startling statement, and I quote: 'We are therefore forced to contemplate the fact that as much as 90 percent of the matter in the universe is both invisible and quite unknown—perhaps unknowable—to us.'[3]

"Think of that," Anne presses. "We cannot see, feel, or measure most of the universe. Does that sound like anything we Latter-day Saints know about? About the time I was reading this book, my grandfather, Theodore Rosenstadt, died. I was very close to him, and so I thought about him a lot after his passing. I wondered where he went and how it was possible that he could be close and not be observed in some way. I was fascinated by the possibilities when I read Smoot's statement, 'As much as 90 percent of the matter in the universe is both invisible and quite unknown—perhaps unknowable—to us.' What a discovery—a possible scientific explanation of the spirit world! Now, I know this is idle speculation, but I just wanted you to see how my mind works.

"I've got to keep moving here or Brother 'M' is going to cut me off," she states, glancing over at Brother Matthews.

"No, Anne," he replies, "I can see that you're just getting started, and you are generally on the subject, so please continue."

Anne seems to pick up the pace even more and says, "Now, what I really want you to think about is this: We on good old planet Earth are pretty self-centered. Still, I want to put our position in perspective. Heavenly Father, while dealing with us each individually, has a lot on his mind. For example, we are floating around a pretty mediocre star called the sun. We are at the distant outskirts of a rather ordinary galaxy called the Milky Way. I remember when I was somewhat younger, looking at the Milky Way in the night sky and appreciating its beauty. It wasn't until I was a little older that

I found out I was *living* inside the Milky Way. Even then, it was a little difficult to understand how I could be seeing it and be a part of it at the same time!"

The class laughs softly and Anne smiles, then continues.

"I later learned that the Milky Way galaxy is filled with an estimated 200 billion stars. I can't even comprehend that number. Most of these stars are more significant in size and brightness than the sun. Truly, we're living in a nondescript solar system. If we didn't live here, no one would notice this insignificant planet. But, regarding this seemingly ordinary solar system, Heavenly Father made an interesting choice. He placed a humongous quantity of his children within it. Then he placed his firstborn son in a backwater Galilean town named Nazareth. That didn't happen, however, until the Son was born in a manger in an obscure village called Bethlehem.

"Are you getting the picture here?" Anne asks, looking intently at each of the faces before her. (Of course, she can't see *our* faces, because we are hidden in the back of the room, probably made up of the stuff George Smoot talked about. As authors, we're not sure if imagination is part of that hidden material—but who knows?)

Surprisingly, Anne suddenly seems to shift into an even higher gear, and adds, "Now, if what I have been telling you about was the end of it, that would still be pretty amazing. How does Heavenly Father keep track of us one by one while keeping up with the management of 200 billion stars in the Milky Way? Before you answer, let me take it even further. As you may have guessed, the Milky Way is a rather insignificant galaxy in the cosmic scheme of things. When we stare into the night sky, we see hundreds of pinpoints of fire. Some of these are stars and some of these are galaxies. Beyond our visual range are hundreds of thousands of galaxies. To challenge your thinking further, let me add that some have estimated that there are at least 100 billion galaxies in the universe, maybe even more. One more thing—the average galaxy contains 100 billion stars.

"Now," Anne continues, her brow furrowing, "I'm not trying to confuse matters, as they are already complicated enough. I am simply trying to tell you about the condescension of God. In the midst of the complex universe, he hears and answers our prayers, sends his love, comforts us when we're sad, and shows interest in the things we're interested in. In other words, he really *knows* us and *loves* us!

"Brothers and sisters," she concludes, smiling warmly, "I'm supposed to close tonight with these verses from 1 Nephi 11. Let's prepare for the verse by thinking about the following question: Can any demonstration of condescension be more profound than the one shown to Nephi when the angel said: 'Look and behold the condescension of God! And I looked and beheld the Redeemer of the world, of whom my father had spoken. . . . And I beheld that he went forth ministering unto the people, in power and great glory; and the multitudes were gathered together to hear him; and I beheld that they cast him out from among them. . . . And I, Nephi, saw that he was lifted up upon the cross and slain for the sins of the world.'" (Verses 26–27, 28, 33.)

Sensing that she had underscored her point, Anna bore a short testimony and then sat down. Without editorializing on her remarks, Brother Matthews simply called on a young man named Raul Davis to pray, and the class was dismissed.

As we thought about the ideas presented in this chapter, it is obvious to us that the condescension of God is manifest in his love for his children. If all of us are to ever fully understand the Atonement or his grace in relationship to our exaltation, we must deepen our comprehension of his condescension.

We would like to put this discussion in perspective by drawing your attention to these truths: God the Son, the creator of this world and the author of our salvation, condescended to come to Earth. This he did to take upon him flesh and to take upon himself our sins, our sorrows, our pains, our mistakes, and our infirmities. From the beginning, it always has been and will be by his grace that we are ultimately saved in the kingdom of God. Our works will always be assisted by him and should be an outward expression of our profound and eternal gratitude for his grace.

We know that the Lord's tender mercies are, in fact, expressed in his creations. In the words of a tender parent, he said to us: "This is my work and my glory—to bring to pass the immortality and eternal life of man" (Moses 1:39).

We are also discovering that one important ingredient in the process of understanding the Atonement and grace is to begin to appreciate the meaning of the question posed to Nephi in his marvelous vision—"Knowest thou the condescension of God?" (1 Nephi 11:16.)

_____NOTES

1. Dietrich Bonhoeffer, *The Cost of Discipleship* (New York: Macmillan Publishing Co., 1963), p. 99.

2. See Stephen Hawking, *A Brief History of Time* (New York: Bantam, 1988).

3. George Smoot, *Wrinkles in Time* (New York: William Morrow and Co., 1993), p. 164.

CHAPTER NINE

Putting Grace in Place:
Tendering a Contrite Spirit

We previously discussed the importance and effect of a broken heart upon our developing a clear understanding of the power of the Savior's grace. Although all do not have the same experiences, the Savior made it clear that a "broken heart and a contrite spirit" are essential requirements of the gospel (see 3 Nephi 9:20). To be contrite implies many things, but generally it includes feeling remorse or sorrow, being willing to listen or change, desiring reconciliation, and so on. One with a truly contrite spirit is more likely to hear and obey promptings from heaven.

Mormon, the great Nephite prophet, teaches us what being contrite is *not*. In the record of his life he describes the deepening depravity of his people. In Mormon 2 he states that "wickedness did prevail upon the face of the whole land . . . and the work of miracles and of healing did cease because of the iniquity of the people. . . . And the Holy Ghost did not come upon any, because of their wickedness and unbelief." (Verses 13, 14.)

Mormon continues this tragic tale of needless tribulation, telling us that at one time the destructive effects of the wars with the Lamanites led his people to moments of deep despair. When at first it appeared to their leader that they were finally yielding to the Spirit, he rejoiced in their apparent contrition. His excitement was short-lived, however, as he wrote these woeful words: "But behold this my joy was vain, for their sorrowing was not unto repentance, because of the goodness of God; but it was rather the sorrowing of the damned, because the Lord would not always suffer them to take happiness in sin. And they did not come unto Jesus with *broken hearts and contrite spirits*, but they did curse God, and wish to die. . . . And I saw that *the day of grace was passed* with them." (Mormon 2:13–15.)

It is hard for the righteous to imagine such a condition in either an individual or a whole society, although it may well be happening before our eyes in modern times.

A contrast to Mormon's description is Elder Boyd K. Packer's portrait of the work of the Spirit upon a truly contrite heart. He states:

> Obedience—that which God will never take by force—He will accept when freely given. And he will then return to you freedom that you can hardly dream of—the freedom to feel and to know, the freedom to do, and the freedom to *be*, at least a thousandfold more than we offer Him. Strangely enough, the key to freedom is obedience.
>
> I would expose you . . . to some tender, innermost feelings on this matter of agency. Perhaps the greatest discovery of my life, without question the greatest commitment, came when finally I had the confidence in God that I would loan or yield my agency to Him—without compulsion or pressure, without any duress, as a single individual alone, by myself, no counterfeiting, nothing expected other than the privilege. In a sense, speaking figuratively, to take one's agency, that precious gift which the scriptures make plain is essential to life itself, and say, 'I will do as thou directs,' is afterward to learn that in so doing you possess it all the more.[1]

The surrendering of our will to God's may happen in a variety of ways. We are deeply grateful to Elder Robert E. Wells of the Quorum of the Seventy for sharing a singularly personal experience that illustrates a path one person took which eventually resulted in such a yielding of the will. This process also brought in its wake a profound discovery concerning the doctrine of grace and the Savior's tender mercies to his children. The following is from a transcript of a tape made by Elder Wells for his family, and we thus conclude this chapter in his words:

> I grew up in Las Vegas, Nevada. Prior to my going into military service, I fell hopelessly in love with a beautiful young lady, Meryl Leavitt. We had dated on and off for several years—even during the time I was in the Navy and when I was attending Brigham Young University. In addition, Meryl was the only person who sent me money with every letter during my mission. So with this much time and energy invested in me, she felt that she had a claim on me.
>
> When PacifiCorp offered me an international banking job back in Latin America, where I had served my mission, I considered all of the girls I had dated. I knew that Meryl was the only one with the character and ability to handle an international banking lifestyle. She was a solid Latter-day Saint—a Golden Gleaner, a returned lady missionary—and had all the qualities I was looking for in an eternal companion.
>
> In addition, Meryl was very much a country girl, raised on a farm near Las Vegas. She drove a truck and handled horses like she was born to a saddle, yet was sophisticated and strikingly beautiful. In short, she was very much at home wearing Levi's in a corral or wearing evening gowns as a city girl.
>
> So in 1953, we married in the Salt Lake Temple, then moved immediately back to Buenos Aires, Argentina, and to my new career there. At that time I insisted that Meryl take flying lessons, since flying small aircraft was one of my greatest passions. She eagerly complied and began taking lessons from an Argentine instructor. We piloted together, and before long she had passed her written and flying exams.
>
> We then moved from Argentina to Uruguay and purchased a Cessna 170 tail-wheel airplane. We actually purchased it back in Las Vegas, and after test-driving it across the country to New York, we flew it back to Uruguay. This plane cost us four thousand dollars and was actually paid for out of my travel expense reimbursement from the bank.
>
> We did quite a bit of flying with that aircraft. Then, when we were transferred up to Paraguay by the bank to open a Citicorp branch there, we sold this first plane. Over the next several years we purchased three more planes, flying them literally over the countries of South America. By this time we had

three lovely children, and I was either serving as a branch or a district president in the Church. The entire world seemed to be at our beck and call.

On one occasion, in 1960, when we were in the United States, a problem occurred with our Piper Comanche. My partner in this plane had rented it out to a friend of his, and this friend had run it off a runway into a ditch. The right landing gear had broken off, and since the plane was not covered by insurance, my partner's friend agreed to pay for the repairs. The repairs on the plane were made, and both Meryl and I flew it several times in order to make sure everything was functioning properly.

During those years I had also been giving additional flight training to Meryl, and in essence had become her advanced cross-country flight instructor. She was a marvelous pilot too and had a sixth sense about how to respond to given situations—even instrument flying.

After we had determined that this plane was in perfect flying condition, we decided to fly from our home in Paraguay to Buenos Aires, Argentina, and attend an opera there. We would take two other couples with us and fly two planes, and afterward we would fly over to Uruguay to attend a Church conference there. President and Sister Joseph Fielding Smith were to be in attendance, so the trip loomed as a cultural and spiritual feast.

We had a great flight to Argentina, attended the opera, then flew to Uruguay to the Church meeting. We had planned on staying for the Sunday morning conference session, then fly home. There was a bad-weather report, however, so we felt we should leave in the morning rather than wait until after the Church meetings.

To this point, both of our planes were performing perfectly. We had flown from Asuncion, Paraguay, the one thousand miles down to Buenos Aires. I was flying a friend's Cessna 182 with tricycle gear, and Meryl was flying our less-powered Piper Comanche. The Comanche had a one thousand mile traveling capacity, however, so the two planes could fly together in loose formation.

We flew partway home, then had to land and refuel in the northern part of Uruguay. By now, however, the weather had improved, and our destination point was clear. The country was flat, and we could enjoy a leisurely flight back to Paraguay.

By this time Meryl had begun having intermittent problems with her radio. Often when she called from her plane to mine, her voice would be garbled. We flew approximately two city blocks apart, and because the planes had flashing strobe lights, we were able to keep track of each other.

Shortly after taking off from our refueling station, I found myself looking up through a hole in the clouds. I knew that I could fly up through this small opening and see if it was all right for us to fly between the layers of clouds. I reasoned that there would be less turbulence at that higher altitude.

I made it up through the clouds, then radioed to Meryl to have her follow. She didn't immediately answer, however, but after a minute or so of silence I heard her garbled transmission. She was saying that she had lost visual contact with me. I replied by instructing her to go back down and fly beneath the layer of clouds. This was the last communication we had between each other. We had previously agreed that if her radio went out, we would meet up again at the next airport, in Corrientes, Argentina. This was about an hour's flight from where we then were. We each had two people with us to keep us company, so I didn't feel too concerned for her at that time.

I thus continued flying until I arrived in Corrientes. I did advise the Uruguay tower at our refueling station that I had lost contact with Meryl and that I was proceeding on to our rendezvous point.

When I landed in Corrientes, the officials there informed me that Meryl's plane had indeed crashed, and that it had been found. They also stated that there were survivors but that I would need to return to the crash site for further information.

Leaving my two passengers in Corrientes to catch a commercial flight back home, I immediately flew back toward Uruguay. I landed without incident in Concordia, where I had been told that Meryl had crashed; but no one was there to greet me. Within minutes, however, a policeman arrived to pick me up, and then the two of us drove to the crash site. The officer wouldn't tell me anything about the accident but said that I would need to wait until we arrived at the scene to find out the details.

When I pulled up next to the plane, a flatbed truck was there with three obvious bodies rolled in canvas in the back of it. Although it was difficult for my mind to grasp what I was seeing, I knew at that moment that Meryl and the others had perished in the crash, and that the love of my life was now gone from my side. Words will forever be inadequate in expressing the pain that swelled within me, consuming my emotions and numbing my senses. Within me, the profound tears of sorrow simply wouldn't stop flowing.

As my mind attempted to deal with the devastating realization of Meryl's passing, I found myself experiencing tremendous guilt for having somehow caused the crash. Upon further investigation it was determined that there were three possible explanations for the crash: First, the plane's previous runway accident had caused internal metal "fatigue." This fatigue, or crack, could have been detected had we taken the plane to Argentina for a "magna-flux," or a type of X-ray that would have detected the crack.

This explanation seemed likely since the right wing of the plane had actually come off the plane, causing the crash. The wing had broken the tail wing off as well, and so the plane had descended in three separate pieces. The irony of the crash was that the fuselage where Meryl and the others were sitting had landed upright, as though it had experienced a perfect landing.

The three passengers were still strapped in their seats, and according to the attending physician, the impact of the crash had simply snapped their heads down, breaking their necks. Other than that, they had no further bruises. The accident had been a fluke, to be sure, but had happened because of the wing weakening and coming off. From what I could determine, the wing had separated at the exact location where it had previously been repaired.

So, one explanation for the crash was that I had not been prudent in insisting on an X-ray of the plane parts after the runway accident. Another explanation was that Meryl had been unable to follow me up through the hole in the clouds. The hole may have closed in on her since she was not able to climb as fast as I was able to. Her plane simply didn't have the power that mine had. Lastly, Meryl could have made the fatal mistake of not making the transition of trying to follow my plane to flying by her instruments. I knew that if the correct transition from visual to instrument piloting was not made, within seconds the plane could go into what is called a "graveyard spiral." In this case, the nose drops, speed is gathered, and the plane would be unable to pull out of it. If this had happened, the wing could have been pulled off by the sheer force of the angled descent.

In either case, I had not given Meryl adequate instrument flying instructions. Nor had I taken proper precautions in seeing that the metal wing structure was sound. So I was guilty of neglect—and this guilt, combined with the remorse and loss of two dear friends in addition to my beloved childhood sweetheart, became almost more than I could bear. Once the tears stopped, I simply lost my desire to continue on.

The most difficult moment, of course, came when I had to tell our children of their mother's death. Meryl's younger sister, Lynn Leavitt, had been staying with us for the previous three months, and so when I returned to our home, she was the one I told first. She was devastated as well, but somehow she had the strength to help me bring our children together so that I could tell them what had happened. Susan, our eldest, was seven; Bobby was four; and David, our baby, had just turned one.

I knelt down to be on their level, and then, through unabashed tears, I told them of Meryl's accident. When I announced to them that their mother had left us and was once again living with Heavenly Father and Jesus, Susan ran to me and threw her arms around me. Bobby also came to me, and the two of them consoled *me*. This response was entirely unexpected, as I had anticipated being the one to comfort them. Through my tears I was able to tell them that their mother was still alive and that we would once again be together as a family. These words brought with them a reassurance for each of us, although the loss of our sweetheart, sister, and mother was a profoundly lonely and encompassing emotion.

The Lord works miracles, however, because through fervent prayer I was somehow given the strength to take Meryl's remains back to the States for burial. I was also able to continue to care for our three children, as difficult as that was.

Following Meryl's funeral, and after returning to Paraguay with the three children, my mind went into a dark daze. I became a walking vegetable, being able to function only on a minimal level. This I did for the sake of the children, and for no other reason. Truly, I didn't see "in color" for the next year. Everything I saw was in "black and white" and had no beauty to it. I simply existed—nothing more.

Then one evening, while on my knees in prayer, a further miracle occurred. While praying and pleading to my Heavenly Father, I felt as though the Savior came to my side and saved me. He spoke these words to my soul: *"Robert, my atoning sacrifice paid for your sins and your mistakes; and this was a mistake, and Meryl forgives you. Because of this, you have nothing to worry about."*

From that moment, the burden of guilt was amazingly lifted from me. I immediately understood the encompassing power of the Savior's atonement, and I now had a testimony that it applied directly to me. While I had previously felt like I could have been swallowed up to destruction, I now realized that Christ had saved me and that I could enjoy the eternities with my sweetheart, Meryl, and our three beautiful children. At that moment, the tears flowed freely once again—only this time they were tears of happiness, and of hope.

What I was then given was instantaneous and permanent. Just as my mind and emotions had been at the darkest level, I now experienced light and joy like I had never before known. As my mind assimilated what had transpired, I realized that I had been given an unearned gift—the Lord's unearned gift of grace. I didn't deserve it, I had done nothing to merit it, but he gave it to me nonetheless.

As I arose from my knees that night, I knew that my future would be charted and that the Lord would bring a woman into my life and into my home who could fulfill the needs of my family, just as Meryl had done. This knowledge gave me great hope, and before long I had journeyed back to the States in search of her. That was when the tender mercies of the Lord showered down upon me again and I met my beautiful wife, Helen, and our lovely daughter, Dana. Helen has since that time become the mother of three additional daughters and has been the most marvelous helpmeet a man could ever hope for. But that is another story—a beautiful one made possible by the atoning sacrifice of my Lord, and his unconditional gift of grace.

_____Notes

1. Boyd K. Packer, *"That All May Be Edified"* (Salt Lake City: Bookcraft, 1982), pp. 256–57.

CHAPTER TEN

Reflecting on His Grace

By way of review, Brent shares the following personal experience:

In considering the central role of the Savior in our lives, my mind has gone back to the time nearly a decade ago when I visited my folks on their mission in Paris, Tennessee. I traveled with them across the border into Kentucky, where we visited an antique store. There I purchased an old set of keys for one of my children to add to his sense of history.

I also purchased for myself a two-hundred-year-old carpenter's hammer. It presently adorns a prominent shelf in my den, and I think of it often. As I am writing this I have stopped to look at and hold the hammer. In doing so I am reminded of the words of Alma the Younger as recorded in Alma 17:9, 11. They speak of the missionary work of Alma's brethren, the sons of Mosiah—Ammon, Aaron, Omner, and Himni. Let me share these two verses with you:

> And it came to pass that they journeyed many days in the wilderness, and they fasted much and prayed much that the Lord would grant unto them a portion of his Spirit to go with them, and abide with them, that they might be an *instrument* in the hands of God to bring, if it were possible, their brethren, the Lamanites, to the knowledge of the truth. . . .

And the Lord said unto them also: Go forth among the
Lamanites, thy brethren, and establish my word; yet ye shall be
patient in long-suffering and afflictions, that ye may show forth
good examples unto them in me, and I will make an *instrument*
of thee in my hands unto the salvation of many souls.

I have emphasized the word *instrument* in both verses.
Let me now create a metaphor. I will liken my hammer unto
the sons of Mosiah. The unmentioned carpenter, of course, is
the Carpenter of Galilee—Jesus Christ.

Relating this scripture to our own day, if we are to be the
Lord's instruments, we must allow the Master Carpenter to
take us in hand. Then we can assist him in his work. Our
"nails," such as the scriptures or our testimonies, are those
things we use to penetrate the hearts of those whose lives we
are helping him fashion.

So now, as I think of my antique carpenter's hammer, I
think of myself, and you, all of us. I try to serve the Lord in
whatever capacity he may call me to, be it Gospel Doctrine
instructor, deacon's quorum advisor, high councilor, ward
clerk, and so forth. You who are reading this no doubt try to
serve faithfully wherever you are called. What comfort we
each should take in spending part of each day in the service
of the Master! The crucial thing for us to remember, of course,
is that we are simply the hammer; *not* the Master Carpenter.
In understanding the concept of grace, we must never confuse our efforts as a hammer, or instrument, with the mighty
arm of the Savior.

Now, using this metaphor as a base, let me share some
thoughts about parables.

On one occasion while staying with Don's family in
Boston, I visited the Lowell Massachusetts Branch. The
Gospel Doctrine class was taught by Sister Irene Danjou, and
I soon found that she was a gifted teacher. In referring to her
New Testament Gospel Doctrine teacher's supplement, she
indicated that, in all, the Savior introduced and taught ap-
proximately forty parables![1] I'd never known that before. I
was even more impressed when she related that, although
Joseph Smith didn't author any parables himself, he did pro-

vide five of them from the Lord. These were revealed in sections 38, 88, and 101 of the Doctrine and Covenants.

After listening to Sister Danjou, I thought about a parable that Don shared with me two decades ago. While teaching junior high school seminary in Salt Lake City, Don held a year-end testimony meeting with all of his students. During the meeting he became increasingly embarrassed as the students focused on him, their "wonderful teacher," and on his "marvelous works," rather than on the Savior. Don was the only seminary teacher at that junior high school, and he knew that his students really couldn't compare him with any other seminary teachers.

Halfway into the meeting, as he was fidgeting in discomfort, a parable entered his mind. This story is not one that he has told often, but in this context it appears to fit. Together we have further sculpted it in order to give it a broader application and to add clarity. We include it for your consideration:

The Parable of the Young Man and the Garden

There was once a young man who stood outside the walls of a beautiful botanical garden. As he gazed through the fence, he admired this garden and longed to work among the flowers and shrubs growing there. Without the young man's being aware, the master of the garden came near. The master of the garden, sensing this young man's interest in the work, invited him to come and labor in the garden.

"I can't possibly help you," the young man exclaimed. "I have no tools and no skill."

The master of the garden quietly reassured him, saying, "I will give you tools and will teach you the required skills."

The young man agreed to work, and after a period of instruction he was led to a place in the garden. It was in a mature section of the garden, filled with rosebushes that had been planted years before. These full-grown plants had been well cared for and needed only modest trimming. Indeed, it was a good place for the inexperienced young man to begin his apprenticeship.

The young man carefully followed the instructions of the master gardener, trimming the rosebushes, then loosening the soil near the roots.

In a short period of time, the rosebushes began to bud and then to blossom. As the buds burst open and became blossoming roses of many colors, each flower seemed to want to thank the young man for his efforts on its behalf. The young man was quick to resist and explained that when he first came into the garden, he had no tools and no gardening skills.

"Surely," he replied, "I am not responsible for your growth and your beauty. You were planted long ago and have been nurtured and pruned these many years, while only recently did I begin my work with each of you. In truth," he concluded, "even though it may have taken a few days longer, you would have blossomed had I not even entered the garden. We owe all of this—your beauty and my experience of watching the miracle of your blossoming—to the master of the garden. Perhaps one day I may even be entrusted with my own garden."

The roses, now in full and radiant bloom, appeared to acknowledge the words of the young man. Truly, this day had been one of giving and receiving by the young man, the flowers, and the master of the garden.

One of the many results of maturing in the gospel is that we have increasing comprehension of all the Savior does to help us in our labors. Like the young man in the parable, we are not alone in the Master's work, nor do we save ourselves by doing his work. As we perform true works of grace, he is participating with us. While it is true that we exercise our will, we cannot do his work without him.

Consider also the metaphor of each of us being a perennial of great potential in the Savior's garden. As we grow in our understanding of Christ's central role in our daily and eternal lives, we begin to acknowledge all that he does relative to our deep and anchoring root systems. We somehow begin to understand his efforts and energies toward our developing into productive, blossoming flowers. By comparison, we do very little to plant or nurture the other perennials in the garden around us. The Savior, in truth, makes it *all* possible.

———Notes

1. See New Testament Gospel Doctrine Teacher's Supplement, 1987, p. 47.

PART 3

A Change of Behavior:
Once I Understand
His Grace, How Can
I Secure It?

Remembering our discussion at the end of part 1, you can see that we are now in the action phase of the four-step process. Let us now take another look at how the Lord labors with us and for us.

How does the Lord work with us? He commands, and we try to obey. We feel that we're making progress. Then, without warning, our lives suddenly turn upside down. A hurricane out at sea causes pounding waves of turmoil to engulf us. In the midst of this chaos, we become frustrated by our inability to obey everything all the time—especially while we're taking in great gulps of ocean water not of our own choosing.

In our fears and anxieties, we turn to the Lord. This time, however, we really do it with all our hearts!

To assist in the understanding of this evolutionary change process, imagine a conversation between our Heavenly Father and an individual who is trying hard but feels real frustration. The dialogue might go something like this:

What Is the Heart of My Part?

"I cannot get this all together all the time," I say.

The Lord says, "Remember my words: 'Come unto me, all ye that labour and are heavy laden, and I will give you rest' (Matthew 11:28).

" 'Come unto me all ye ends of the earth, buy milk and honey, without money and without price' (2 Nephi 26:25). Yield your heart to me now," he adds, "and you will be accepted."

"I am not rebellious," I reply, "and I don't commit major transgressions. Still, I commit less serious sins and I make what seems like innumerable mistakes in failing to always do your will."

"If you yield your heart to me, your desire to commit sin will continue to diminish, and your strength to resist will increase."

"But sometimes I stray a little and get out of tune . . ."

"If you stray too far, you may lose your way and your sense of belonging; so be careful. When you stray, repent quickly, and continue to yield your heart to me."

"But," I ask, "when can I have assurance that I will return to be with you?"

"When you are penitent and yield your heart."

"I have feelings of being penitent and a desire to yield my heart now—almost all the time."

"I believe you."

"Then does that mean that it is safe to feel accepted and assured now?" I ask. "I need to know!"

"Yes, as long as you continue to proceed in this path," he reassures me. "However, you will necessarily feel some pain and discomfort within you as you respond to the encouragement and direction of the Holy Spirit, which entices you to change and to improve."

"I thought I had to do it alone and that your grace took effect only after I had done all I could possibly do!"

"My child, you know by your own experience that I have been with you—encouraging you and opening the way—for as long as you can remember."

"Why haven't these things been this clear before?" I wonder out loud.

"You weren't prepared to receive them," is his kind response.

"Is this like the concept of 'cheap grace'?" I ask.

"Not even remotely so, because it is not up to me alone or to you alone. We are partners in all of your efforts to return home," he says encouragingly.

"Then when I have yielded my heart completely—unconditionally—what must I do?" I ask, listening more fervently than ever.

"You must be continuously involved in the work of grace."

"I don't understand." I try to comprehend his words. "If it is work, how can it be grace? And if it is grace, how can it be work?"

"You must now carefully read my words in the Doctrine and Covenants—section 93 verses 1 through 20," he counsels. "Once you have read these words, you must reflect upon them. I will then give you the enabling power to understand them, as I season you and encourage you along your life's path."

It is true that the information contained in Doctrine and Covenants 93:1–20 has significant meaning in relation to the whole doctrine of grace. As the two of us have discussed these verses over the years, we have felt a deepening of our understanding of his grace and how it operates. The discussions provided insights and the basis for defining moments of discovery that changed our lives. We now invite you now to look at section 93 with us.

CHAPTER ELEVEN

Grace for Grace:
Participating in the Work of Grace

Brother Randy Thomas is at the door greeting the group as they file into the Relief Society room where the Gospel Doctrine class is held. Moving to the front, he says to all of them, "It is my pleasure to welcome you back to class."

As you can see, we have returned to our fictional Sunday School class in order to observe their final discussion on the doctrine of grace. We think you are all accustomed to sneaking in like this, so we needn't remind you to be quiet while we listen. Due to stake conference, there has been a two-week break since the last class. Some individual discussions have taken place in the interim. We, of course, listened in on the one between Tom Wilson and David Bradley. These two brethren are present, along with most of those who attended the earlier classes. Let's listen now as Brother Thomas is getting started.

Following a brief introduction, he moves to the lesson. "As most of you know, two weeks ago we said we would spend one more class period on the subject of grace. I want to use section 93 in the Doctrine and Covenants as a starting point for today's discussion.

"I asked Sister Judy Hansen to give a brief explanation about the origin and content of this section. Judy, please."

Moving quickly to the front of the class, Judy introduces her presentation by saying, "I spent quite a bit of time this week reading and pondering the revelation as recorded in D&C 93. Some gospel scholars have said that this was one of the most profound revelations Joseph ever received.

"One of the remarkable things I discovered was that Joseph Smith was only twenty-seven years of age when he received this revelation. That astonishes me, given its profound content. He also recorded section 94 on the same day. The more I learn about Joseph Smith, the more I realize that he had an almost unequalled capacity to know the Lord's will.

"If I understand the information in section 93 correctly, I've learned that grace also applied in the life of the Savior. I had never considered that *he* was influenced by the grace of the Father too!"

"What do you mean, Judy?" Tom Wilson interrupts. "I'm not sure I follow you."

"Just this: Even as we must do, Christ the Lord likewise went through progressive stages of suffering and obeying until finally he was prepared to return to the presence of the Father—and of course to receive of the Father's fulness.

"Although the process he went through has many vital differences from what we encounter, there are also some significant similarities. For example, he received not a fulness at first, but afterward did receive it."

"I don't understand exactly what you're saying, Judy," comes another comment from among the group.

"Well, perhaps an easier way to understand this is for us to read the passage together. Please, all turn to D&C 93 verses 12 and 13, and could I have a volunteer read for us?"

Vaughn Rasmussen offers and then begins reading: " 'And I, John, saw that he received not of the fulness at first, but received *grace for grace;* and he received not of the fulness at first, but continued from *grace to grace,* until he received a fulness.' "

"Before we go on," Judy continues, "can you see that according to these verses, Christ received grace as he gave it? Any comments?"

David Bradley, the patriarch, raises his hand. When
called upon, he makes this observation: "It seems to me that
there was a process going on here, not a series of isolated
events. The reason for making that distinction comes from an
idea that I have been developing. I think grace is as much
about who we are becoming as it is about what we are doing.
As Christ, the Son, gave gifts of his time, his life, and his love,
the Father added grace to the Son. This is what we must do,
and what we will receive."

Continuing, Brother Bradley says, "I need to add a comparison here, however. Christ was baptized to 'fulfill all
righteousness.' On the other hand, I was baptized, in part, for
a remission of my sins. These are fundamentally different
reasons for the same act. In the case of Christ receiving 'grace
for grace,' this process is not one-to-one the same for us. It is,
however, a pattern which we must follow."

At this point, Judy gently interrupts. "Now, Brother
Bradley," she admonishes, smiling, "you're getting a little
ahead of us. In verses 19 and 20 we're given additional information and instructions concerning the process of receiving
grace for grace, and for progressing from grace to grace.
Vaughn, please read those two verses."

" 'And I give unto you these sayings that you may understand and know *how to worship*, and know *what you worship*,
that you may come unto the Father in my name, and in due
time receive of his fulness. And if you keep my commandments you shall receive of his fulness, and be glorified in me
as I am in the Father; therefore, I say unto you, you shall receive *grace for grace.*' "

"Thank you, Vaughn," Judy says. "I want to emphasize the
importance of the two phrases in verse 19 that say 'know how
to worship' and 'know what you worship.' The message in
these verses is beyond the scope of our discussion today, but I
would encourage all of us to ponder the meaning of these
phrases. Getting on to verse 20, brothers and sisters, this verse
seems to imply that being saved by grace includes my performing grace, or my rendering gifts of service to others—gifts
they have not earned. It is through this process of giving of
myself to others, developing a life of grace, that I may be transformed until, like Christ, I receive of the fulness of the Father.

"Now, one final thought: Although a strict reading of the words in this section may seem to imply that grace occurs in each single act or giving of service, I, too, believe that grace is more completely defined by what I am becoming rather than just by what I am doing."

As Judy finishes speaking, she turns to the instructor, Brother Thomas, and says, "This is my understanding of section 93 verses 1 through 20 and its prominent concepts."

Brother Thomas walks again to the front of the room. After thanking Judy for an excellent presentation, he asks Tom Wilson to come forward. While Tom is coming to the front of the class, Brother Thomas says, "During the past two weeks one of our class members, Brother Wilson, has been very busy. He spent an evening at the Bradleys' talking about grace and then a few days later came by to see me. I have asked him and two others to give presentations concerning the process of receiving grace for grace. Now, I don't want to add a lot of commentary on these stories. I think they are self-explanatory. Tom, why don't you start?"

Tom Wilson comes to the front of the room carrying a rolled-up copy of a national magazine. "I recently purchased this magazine," he tells the group. "I had heard about an article in it titled 'Saving Grace,' and I wanted to share it with you. It is the story of an eighty-seven-year-old black woman by the name of Osceola McCarty. She lived her entire life in Hattiesburg, Mississippi, without marrying. She began washing clothes by hand when she was just a little girl. She did this throughout her life and never did purchase a washing machine. Instead, she used a scrub board, and became very well known for the services she provided.

"A few months ago, this Ms. McCarty donated her life savings of about $150,000 to the University of Southern Mississippi, to be used to finance scholarships for the community's African-American students. She said that she wanted others to have what she could not have—a real chance at education.

"Isn't that amazing," Tom exclaims, "that this woman could support herself washing clothes by hand and save that much money—not to mention that she would give it away to people she doesn't even know. What makes this story even more complete is what happened *after* she gave her gift. Local businessmen in her community have now pledged to match her $150,000 in the same scholarship fund. Since that time, additional fund-raising has significantly added to the total.

"Brothers and sisters," Tom concludes, "many of you know that I have had some trouble with the definition and application of the doctrine of grace in the Church. I chose this particular story to illustrate my changing understanding of grace. I wanted to focus on the other side of grace, our side of the 'grace for grace' equation. 'What must I do to receive his grace?' was the question I kept asking myself. It has finally dawned on me that I must become like the Savior in giving myself away to others. This is not merely a series of acts of service, but rather a conversion of my innermost self.

"I also think I should say that I certainly am not all the way there. Total conversion of my inner person is my goal, and I am making real progress. What has really helped is knowing that I don't have to do this alone. It isn't up to me to do all I can do *first*. Rather, Christ's grace is working upon me all the time. This discovery is one of the most important in my life, and for that I am deeply grateful."

Our instructor, Randy Thomas, walks back to the front of the room and thanks Tom for his insightful presentation. Then he says to the class, "I have asked Sister Anna Dilworth to share with us a wonderful story she discovered while reading the biography of Louisa May Alcott. Sister Anna, would you please come up here to the front to give your report."

You may remember Sister Dilworth from a previous class. She is lovingly called "Sister Anna" by ward members—even though she is in her late seventies. Her health is excellent, given her age, and her mind is as sharp as ever. She loves standing in front of the group, and is given to a little dramatic flair. She begins, "I want to tell you about Bronson and Abba Alcott. Now, you may ask, who in the world are Bronson and Abba Alcott? They are Louisa May Alcott's parents—the Louisa May Alcott who wrote the book *Little Women*. Recently someone gave me a wonderful book titled *Invincible Louisa*, by Cornelia Meigs. It's actually one of the more fascinating biographies I've ever read—and, as you may suspect, I've read a few in my day. But in reading this book I have an entirely new perspective of Louisa May and her family.

"Now," she smiles, "I'd like to share one small incident that may or may not have actually happened, but at least it reflects the outstanding values taught in the Alcott home. It took place while they were living in their home they called the 'Hosmer Cottage' in Concord, Massachusetts, which is where the famed 'Orchard House,' described in the book and movie titled *Little Women*, was also located. Now, if you haven't read the book or seen one of the two movie versions of that story, I won't upbraid you; but I will feel very sorry for you. Rent the video, brethren, and don't be so chauvinistic. Your wives and children will love you for it! But I'm getting away from the story again. Back to *Invincible Louisa.*

"Louisa's father, Bronson, was very trusting in the Lord—to the point of literally and figuratively giving people the shirt off his back. One wintery day the Alcotts, with a young baby in their home, found themselves with almost no fuel. They were blessed to have a caring neighbor bring them a load of wood that would last them through the night.

"Abba, Louisa's mother, was relieved that their prayers had been answered and they could keep the fire going. Later that evening Bronson learned of the needs of a young family who lived nearby. The father of this family told Bronson that they had a sick baby and no fuel. Feeling his natural compassion for another in need, Bronson took the man out to the shed, let him take the wood he needed, and even helped carry it to the family's home.

"Now, Abba, Bronson's wife, was very angry when she found out what he had done. She reminded him that they had a baby as well, and that their home needed to be warm like that of the family he had helped. She was in the process of scolding Bronson, in fact, when there came a knock at the door. As Bronson opened it, he was surprised to greet another of their neighbors, who was unaware of what had just happened but had decided to bring the Alcotts a load of wood. Bronson's response to all of this was that he had trusted that the Lord would take care of the Alcotts."[1]

Finishing her story, Sister Anna determines to make one more comment. "I've lived a long time, during which I have observed people who *know* about the Lord's grace. They are involved in the work of grace in everyday lives. They don't keep score, they just keep at it. I hope that someday I can be like that."

With those tender words spoken, Sister Anna sits down. Everyone knows that Sister Anna is like Bronson Alcott, but she would never say it herself or consider it true.

Brother Thomas again walks back to the front of the room and thanks Sister Anna for sharing the story and her wisdom. Then he does something that seems like pure fantasy. He indicates that he has two special guests from out of town—and he says that their names are Don and Brent. We're not sure how he does this, but he introduces Don, then calls on him to share a final story. He somehow knows that Don can relate a particular incident that applies to the discussion. Don therefore walks to the front of the room. Perhaps Don should relate what happens next:

To tell the truth, I (Don) find myself being surprised that this could be happening; but then, in a book like this, anything is possible! I begin giving a little explanation of who I am. I don't tell the class everything, of course; they wouldn't believe me. As it is, everyone just seems to accept me.

"Brothers and sisters," I begin, "my family and I have lived in New England for about eight years. During our stay there we have met a wonderful family that I would like to tell you about. I wish you could know the people involved, as words will never convey the depth and power of what I have learned from them. They are John and Maryanne Zeller, who live in Duxbury, Massachusetts.

"The Zellers' story began about seventeen or eighteen years ago, when John moved to the Boston area from Utah. He came looking for work. He never returned to Utah, and from what he's told me, he found much more than work in the East. He also found his wife.

"Maryanne came from a wonderful family. Although the rest of her family had not found the gospel, they had discovered many of its principles. Maryanne grew up in a service-oriented home, and her mother had become an angel of mercy in the lives of literally hundreds of disabled youth. At first these impaired young people came into her home as 'wards of the state.' Their disabilities were frequently very severe, causing real hardship on Maryanne's family. Quite often, and in spite of their problems, these children were adopted by Maryanne's parents and become permanent members of the family.

"Not long after arriving in New England, John began to court Maryanne. When he found out about the complexities of her family life, he was put off by the time-consuming emphasis of helping the helpless, but he fell in love with Maryanne anyway. After a beautiful courtship, during which Maryanne joined the Church, John married her. However, he did not fully realize that when a man marries a woman, he also marries her family. In Maryanne's case this old adage was true, and her family was, as I have indicated, plentiful!

"Soon after their marriage, John learned that 'special needs' children consume a great deal of time and energy. There was much caring that had to be expended in their behalf. Marrying into Maryanne's family meant that John had to join in the caring process. At first he was irritated by the imposition this added responsibility made on his time and the distraction it was to his relationship with his new bride. In fact, he simply resented it.

"Some time later, John and Maryanne had a child—a handsome son named Sean. Two years later, a daughter named Katy was born into their family. Upon seeing this newborn child for the first time, it was painfully obvious to her parents that all was not well with her. John was stunned to discover that he had not been sent a perfectly formed child. He sensed that Katy's care would require a great deal of time, and he was again annoyed by the prospects of having to deal with a less-than-perfect family member.

"As John left the hospital, he cried out in his mind, and perhaps aloud, *Lord, why me? Why do I have to have the burden of a Down's syndrome child? Lord, why me?*

"In the years that followed, John and Maryanne spent their days with Katy in the typical parental acts of caring for, nurturing, teaching, and training. For John, it was surprisingly a time of sweet discovery. Loving parents learn to feel that each child, in his or her own way, is a part of the parent. The sincere expressions of love and appreciation returned by children to parents were richly present in John's relationship with Katy. Day after day, in small and large doses, John received much more than he gave.

"As I said before, about eight years ago our family moved into the ward where the Zellers live. I first saw Katy as a Primary child. In my mind's eye I can remember her standing near the front of the group of children when the Primary was asked to perform in sacrament meeting. Looking this way and that, sometimes not fully aware of her role, Katy would sing unrestrained. In doing so, she always tried to position herself near the microphone so that she could be heard. She may have been a little off-key, and may not always have used the right words, but she sang with an infectious enthusiasm that almost hypnotized the congregation.

"Today Katy is a vivacious thirteen-year-old and very much in love with life. She has indeed become a ray of sunshine in our ward. She is innocence wrapped up not in swaddling clothes but in modern teenage attire. We have heard that sometimes we entertain angels unaware. Katy is truly one of those angels.

"I can mentally envision Katy the day she advanced into the Young Women program. A special glow radiated around her. 'I am a Young Woman now,' she exclaimed.

"I can see Katy at her first Young Women basketball game. Dressed as a player, waiting for her turn from the bench, she said little. She somehow understood that Beehives were only allowed to play when the game was no longer in doubt.

"Early in the fourth quarter, when it finally became Katy's turn to play, the score was very lopsided in our ward's favor. She came out onto the floor, play resumed, and soon a teammate passed her the ball. This four-foot-eight-inch bundle of enthusiasm knew nothing about dribbling. She only knew that the crowd cheered loudest when the ball went into the basket.

"So, taking the ball firmly in her hands, Katy bounced it up and down for several seconds, then clutched it tightly in her arms and ran toward a basket.

"Kindly, and with noticeable compassion, the other nine players moved aside. Approaching the basket, Katy clutched the ball in her hands, brought it down by her knees, then threw it as high as she could toward the rim.

"The crowd screamed and applauded while the ball settled softly into the net, then slipped slowly out the bottom for a score!

"At that instant, from the group of spectators sitting on the stage, an anxious mother's voice could be heard. 'Katy,' she called out, 'you put the ball in the wrong basket!'

" 'Oh, Mom,' Katy yelled back, 'it doesn't matter . . . it went in!'

"Many lessons were learned that day; yet for Katy, it was a day she'll likely forget.

"There is not one single story which truly captures the essence of Katy. Her simple life, filled with heroic acts, has a transforming influence upon those closest to her, which cannot be fully expressed in anecdotes. Nevertheless, perhaps another illustration or two will add depth to our understanding.

"At one time, Marybeth, the youngest natural child of the Zellers, listened in a testimony meeting to the words of a member of the ward who had recently given birth to a baby. The woman expressed feelings of gratitude for having been blessed with a healthy child. In fact, the sister spoke of her relief when she found that the baby was normal. The new mother specifically said that she was so grateful that her baby didn't have Down's syndrome.

"Marybeth walked away from the meeting feeling perplexed. When next she spoke to her mother, she asked, 'Mother, why wouldn't everyone want to have the blessing of a Down's syndrome child in their family?'

"In our ward," I continue, "Katy's family is known, with good cause, as the 'service family.' For example, if a family moves in or out of the ward, John and Maryanne, together with their three natural children and their several foster children, go earliest to assist. They don't leave until the bathroom is scrubbed—you know, the last task to be completed, which signifies that the job is really finished.

"I saw John at church one day and asked, 'John, how are things? What's going on?'

"'I can only think of one word,' he replied, smiling, 'I'm content.'

"John recently told me that when he now thinks of the day of Katy's birth, he exclaims in his mind, *Lord, why me? Why am I so blessed to have a Down's syndrome child in my home? Lord, why me?*

"Heavenly Father apparently loved John Zeller so much that, as an act of grace, he gave Katy to him. She *is* an angel— a beautiful raven-haired angel. Now, after developing the same Christlike heart that Maryanne cultivated in her youth, John performs more acts of grace than any man I have ever known. Together, he, Maryanne, and their family make up a team that would capture the gold medal in the World Olympics of Grace! There is never a feeling that they're keeping score. They simply spend their lives performing acts of grace. Heavenly Father's bestowal of grace upon them—like the gift of Katy—flows naturally toward them as soft waves from a calm sea. Surely, heaven would not be complete without them being there."

The class nods in agreement, and I slip to the back of the room. Brother Thomas indicates that he wants to finish the class period with two thoughts. Taking a deep breath, he begins. "I found a quotation from C. S. Lewis in Elder Neal A. Maxwell's book *That My Family Should Partake* that I think may lead us to a possible conclusion about the Lord's grace. C. S. Lewis made a profound observation when considering the implication behind the Savior's cry 'Why has thou forsaken me?' He states: 'There is a mystery here which, even if I had the power, I might not have the courage to explore. Meanwhile, little people like you and me, if our prayers are sometimes granted beyond all hope and probability, had better not draw hasty conclusions to our own advantage. If we were stronger, we might be less tenderly treated. If we were braver, we might be sent, with far less help, to defend far more desperate posts in the great battle.'[2]

"We should not assume," Brother Thomas continues, "that Heavenly Father's grace will always come in the form of relief from trial or difficulty. Surely our friend John Zeller did not see the immediate value of living and working around Maryanne's family. Neither did he initially understand the great blessing that Katy would be in the lives of those around her, particularly his life. 'Grace for grace' is not a simple matter.

"As we continue to fashion our lives after the pattern of the Savior, we shall receive grace *for* grace. We give unearned gifts of love to others. We receive far more from our Father. As we do his work, if we are developing pure motives our acts of charity will not be given for any reasons other than a desire to serve others and help Heavenly Father in the work of grace. As this occurs, we will progress from grace *to* grace."

With this, Brother Thomas calls on someone to pray, and the class ends. Each of those in attendance, including ourselves, leave the room a little more humbled and a little wiser.

_____NOTES

1. See Cornelia Meigs, *Invincible Louisa* (Boston: Little, Brown and Co., 1933), pp. 32–33.
2. As cited in Neal A. Maxwell, *That My Family Should Partake* (Salt Lake City: Deseret Book Co., 1974), p. 85.

CHAPTER TWELVE

In the Footsteps of the Master: From Grace to Grace

Reflecting on a life-changing experience, Brent shares:
I recently returned from a two-week trip to the Holy Land. In conversations with Don, I shared the profound effect this journey to that sacred land had upon me. Because so many impressions about Christ occurred during this remarkable tour, Don suggested that I share some of the feelings that have filled my mind and heart. Before I do that, I want to set the stage.

In the previous chapter we discussed ideas related to the phrase "grace for grace." There is another important phrase in Doctrine and Covenants 93 that adds critical depth to our understanding of the meaning of grace. In verse 13 the Prophet Joseph taught us further about Christ, as follows: "And he received not of the fulness at first, but continued from grace to grace, until he received a fulness."

Our desire in this chapter is to add something to your understanding of the meaning of this verse. Perhaps a little analogy will help. Now, I have great respect for those who are careful users of daily planners. However, it seems that there's a danger inherent in our use of these tools. If we arise in the morning, sit down, and make a list of today's "Acts of Grace to Perform," we're ready for our day, right? We can

120

then go and perform these acts and afterward return home and put a check mark next to each act listed. By this time we've earned the right to serve ourselves a tall glass of lemonade while we sit by the curb waiting for the Heavenly Express delivery truck, as it punctually delivers—by 10:30 P.M., mind you—a package filled with rewards, or acts of grace from our Heavenly Father.

We must be cautious here. In a world that measures everything, that keeps score and constantly looks for winners, it is not surprising, nor is it always inappropriate, that we have a tendency to want to keep track of our accomplishments. However, in the work of grace, if we're not careful we'll go right back to where we started—just performing works to gain a reward, while not allowing our hearts to be transformed. My point is this: grace is not an event but a *condition of the heart*.

Those who are truly engaged in the work of grace will never stand on the shore waiting for blessings to be washed their way with the incoming tide. They just don't feel or act like that. It seems that their caring behavior is caused from within, even though that may sound a little idealistic.

Let me now share my experience in the Holy Land. Our excursion began in Egypt, where my wife, Margaret, and I, along with our eleven-year-old daughter, Angela, ascended to the top of Mount Sinai. We made the three-hour ascent in the dark, then sat at the top and watched the sunrise. As I sat there, meditating in silence, I thought of the great prophet Moses, who, over three millennia earlier, climbed a similar trail. He had then met and conversed with Jehovah, or Christ—the God of the Old Testament. At that point Christ had created worlds without number but had not yet taken on an earthly tabernacle. While most assuredly a god, he had not yet gained the benefits of an earthly existence, nor had he assumed the sins of the world. That event would transpire over twelve hundred years later.

Our journey next took us to the country of Jordan, then across the Jordan River and into the Promised Land. Once there, we went to the northern city of Nazareth, the village of Christ's youth. My mind imagined the young Jesus as he walked the steep and beautiful hills surrounding his early home. He undoubtedly performed acts of grace—however unobserved—as he gained understanding of his identity, then prepared for his ministry.

Traveling up the winding road into Nazareth, we passed within the traditional location of Christ's first public miracle—that of turning water to wine during the wedding feast at Cana. This occurred following Christ's baptism by John the Baptist and after his forty days and nights of fasting. He had withstood the enticements of Lucifer and was thus prepared to begin his three-year public ministry.

The condition of the Savior's heart was never in question. It didn't progress from an irregular beat to one of constancy in service. What it did do, it seems, was enlarge in capacity. Without disobeying, Christ learned obedience. Without misstepping, Christ learned how to walk resolutely forward—even through suffering. These truths are revealed in Paul's epistle to the Hebrews, chapter 5 verses 8 through 10, as follows: "Though he were a Son, yet learned he obedience by the things which he suffered; and being made perfect, he became the author of eternal salvation unto all them that obey him; called of God an high priest after the order of Melchisedec."

It was a wondrous experience for us to then spend several days walking where Jesus walked, while reviewing the events that transpired at each location so long ago. Not only did we rely upon the New Testament authors for this information, but we likewise devoured the impressions and insights of Elder James E. Talmage as recorded in his book *Jesus the Christ*.[1]

From these sources we watched an evolution take place in the Savior's ministry—one increasing in boldness and profound content. Christ ministered daily to those he called his children. He began his ministry by changing water to wine; one of his final miracles was raising Lazarus from the dead. During his three-year public ministry he performed innumerable acts of grace. In all cases the Savior's pure motives, desires, and attitude left the unmistakable handprint of grace. As in his baptism, so in his teachings and his miracles. As in these, so in his stretching to atone for our sins—both in the Garden of Gethsemane as well as on the cross. As in his earthly ministry, so now in ours!

Christ, in a manner we can't duplicate, *did* progress from grace to grace, until in the end he was able to grant us this unearned gift that truly does enable us to follow in his footsteps. It behooves each of us, then, to do as we covenanted to do at the time of our baptism, and then recovenant each week while partaking of the sacrament—that is, to progress from grace to grace by becoming Christlike. Those who discover this often unworn path then internalize the desire to perform acts of grace and are able to quietly and reverently accept the name of Christ for themselves. As followers of Christ, we become his children—an adoption that is essential for those of us who choose inheritance with him in the kingdom of our Father.

Perhaps it would be incomplete for me to leave this discussion of my first journey to the land of our Savior's ministry without sharing what transpired within my all-too-impure heart. While there I found myself seeing the Savior's life in Technicolor rather than in the "black and white" I had been studying during my previous fifty years of living. Even more, I received a layer to my testimony that is difficult for me to share. While in the Garden of Gethsemane, and after I had spoken to our group, I wandered along the path that had been so well prepared for our use. In offering a simple yet honest prayer, I thanked Heavenly Father for sending his Only Begotten into the garden amidst those olive trees, and for allowing Christ to assume the burden of my sins. At that moment, quite unexpectedly, I felt an almost invisible wave of peace pass over me, consuming my entire frame. I knew—more than ever before—that I had been forgiven of my many sins. I knew that the Savior's grace had been personally granted to me; and although I would certainly stumble in the future, acknowledging this heavenly gift was all that mattered at that moment.

For me, it was a new beginning that I have relived in my heart every day since. Now that we have described this critical objective—that of progressing from grace to grace, even as the Lord did while in mortality—let us consider the specific stages of growth and obedience that allow us this blessing.

_____NOTES

1. See James E. Talmage, *Jesus the Christ* (Salt Lake City: Deseret Book Co., 1973).

CHAPTER THIRTEEN

Responding to His Tender Mercies

We the authors know a bishop who was eminently successful in his home teaching efforts. In fact, during his time of service the ward home teaching average was 98.5 percent. Many months, 100 percent home teaching was achieved. This is a remarkable achievement and should give a great deal of satisfaction to both the bishop and the ward members. Imagine—so many families visited by the priesthood each and every month! Not long ago, in a conversation with the bishop, he expressed an insightful concern about his performance in leading the ward to home teaching excellence. He indicated that as he looked upon that achievement, he was concerned about the motives that had been in his heart then. He said that he can remember seeking a high level of performance so that he would impress stake leaders and others who came to visit the stake. He was so driven by that desire that at the end of each month, he and his counselors would actually go out and visit any family that had not yet been home taught. For a bishop to visit families is admirable. For him to visit families for the wrong reason is less desirable.

Now contrast the desire of the bishop with this description of the motivation of the sons of Mosiah as they began their missionary service to the Lamanites: "Now they were desirous that salvation should be declared to every creature, for they could not bear that any human soul should perish; yea, even the very thoughts that any soul should endure endless torment did cause them to quake and tremble" (Mosiah 28:3). Further, the Lord gave counsel to one who apparently had similar motives as the bishop when he said to W. W. Phelps, "And also he hath need to repent, for I, the Lord, am not well pleased with him, for he seeketh to excel, and he is not sufficiently meek before me" (D&C 58:41).

A change of heart is a pivotal result of the influence of the Atonement in our lives. This means a change in our motives, desires, and attitudes. Such a change is of the inner person and is not easily seen by looking at outward performance. Only an omniscient being can determine with certainty the why's of behavior. Nevertheless, it is clear that the Lord expects consistency between *what* we do and *why* we do it. Further, he has let us know that what is happening inside of us, in our hearts, will have a direct bearing on our eternal future.

In a vision the Prophet Joseph Smith saw his brother Alvin residing in the celestial kingdom. He was surprised that his brother was there, because Alvin died before the gospel had been restored. Under the influence of the Spirit, Joseph made these observations:

"All who have died without a knowledge of this gospel, who would have received it if they had been permitted to tarry, shall be heirs of the celestial kingdom of God; . . . for I, the Lord, will judge all men according to their works, according to the desire of their hearts" (D&C 137:7, 9).

At first, such judgment may seem troubling to those who accepted and obeyed the gospel plan in this life. They experienced significant challenges in accepting the gospel and living it. The Lord, however, does not look solely upon the deeds of individuals—he also looks upon their *hearts*. For example, note the Lord's words to the Nephites when he said, "And ye shall offer for a sacrifice unto me a broken heart and a contrite spirit. And whoso cometh unto me with a broken heart and a contrite spirit, him will I baptize with fire and with the Holy Ghost." (3 Nephi 9:20.)

Alma also taught, "None but the truly penitent are saved" (Alma 42:25). Carefully considered, the Lord's ability and willingness to look upon our hearts as well as our deeds should increase our hope and our appreciation for his grace.

As stated earlier, the chapters of this book follow the model shown in chapter 4. That model depicts a four-step process that may help illustrate how we grow in gospel knowledge and gospel living. As you may recall, we suggested that we move within the following pattern: (1) read, (2) reflect, (3) respond, and (4) refine. In part 3 we have been discussing number 3, "Respond." This is the action stage.

From time to time each of us hears or reads of gospel principles that suggest a needed change in our lives. Those who are faithful will try to change in accordance with their understanding of the doctrines that are becoming more clear, while at the same time, the Spirit of the Lord will provide encouragement. Thus, gradual and appropriate change will likely occur.

To make certain that the outcome is what the Lord would have us do, we need to consider not only *what* we do but also *why* we are doing it. Our motives affect the results. Regarding obedience to some gospel principles, our motives for that obedience will not necessarily have a strong effect on the outward performance. However, when we devote ourselves to honest study of the Atonement, the mission of Christ, and the meaning of grace, moments of quiet and profound introspection are created, which will affect our hearts. When our hearts are right and commandments are kept, under the influence of the Lord's Spirit the transformation that creates celestial character occurs. Such a change of heart is, from our understanding, a pivotal ingredient in effective obedience. We think this transformation happens because as we change inside, the quality of our motive for obedience also changes. This refining process will not necessarily produce a pure heart immediately, but when the process is repeated over time, is it not clear that a pure heart will eventually result?

Now, it is not likely that many of us have a single motive for our willingness to keep God's commandments. However, a list of possible motives may help us see how we need to change. The following descriptions, while not exhaustive, are suggestive of why we act the way we do in relationship to gospel obligations and requirements. We are trying here not only to illustrate why we obey but also to show some differences in the gradation or quality of our motivation. Some motives are simply better than others. As we grow in the gospel, with the Lord's help our motives will become better and our behavior will be more like his.

Motivation to Obey

Level one: fear. I obey God because I fear his punishments. I believe that when I disobey, I incur the wrath and punishment of God. The nature of the punishment may be unknown to me, but still, the threat of being punished keeps me in line!

Level two: rewards. I am obedient because, in so doing, I reap the benefits and rewards of keeping the commandments. I may seek the reward of the praise and honor of others. A less troubling illustration of the desire for reward is when I obey because I seek the reward of inheriting the celestial kingdom and of living forever with my eternal companion and my ever-increasing family. (The distinction between these types of reward-seeking may even suggest a separate category or level.)

Level three: love. I love Heavenly Father and Jesus Christ, and I follow them because of this love. I also follow them because they love *me.* I have felt their love through the Holy Spirit, and this feeling inspires and motivates me to become a more obedient son or daughter.

Level four: becoming like them. This may be less a motive than a condition, but it is listed here to illustrate that at the highest possible level my motives will include all that is proper and nothing that is improper. When I become like them, the Father and the Son, we become one—that is, we become one in purpose and power, just as they are one. Just as Christ possesses the fulness of the Father, so will I. At that point, all my behavior is similar to what they would do if they were present.

Additional motives for obedience, such as duty, social pressure (positive and negative), and so forth, might be added to this list. Those listed above were chosen to illustrate the differences in our motives.

Now let us consider the stages of obedience. As we progress from grace to grace, we improve the quality of our obedience. In the illustration that follows, no motives are taken into account, but it is assumed for the sake of discussion that one's motives are progressing properly.

It should be obvious that these stages overlap and may not always happen as described here. But the progress toward a life of service usually includes not doing what is prohibited and also doing what is required. Further, if we get hung up on some of the earlier stages, we may try to get as close to the edge as possible without "really breaking the rules." Or we may bog down in a series of multiplying the commandments—that is, creating our own set of additional commandments. That was the blindness described by Jacob as "looking beyond the mark" (Jacob 4:14). In either event, such foolish behavior is the devil's playground. Honest seekers of truth and righteousness need to maintain what is expected and move on quickly to more significant activities as they are prompted by the Spirit.

Some of the stages of obedience may be expressed as follows:

The Stages of Obedience

Stage one: Obey by not performing the act of transgression. That is, we live the law or rule and thereby eliminate "intentional sin" from our lives.

Stage two: Dutifully keep the commandments—pay tithing, attend meetings, do visiting and home teaching, partake of the sacrament, obey the Word of Wisdom, obey the law of chastity, strive to be totally honest in our dealings with our fellowmen, and so on.

Stage three: Know to do good, and then do it! At this stage we follow the admonition of the Lord in doing "many things of [our] own free will, and [bringing] to pass much righteousness" (D&C 58:27).

Stage four: Seek out opportunities to give service to others. This service may be in the form of helping others find relief from suffering and pain. Such opportunities may also be found in helping others learn and apply gospel principles within the framework of the Lord's church. We may also perform service by doing what we can to bring the saving principles of the gospel to others who do not possess it. In all of these activities we are doing the Lord's work and are involved in the *work* of grace.

Clearly, it is possible to do any of these things for the wrong reasons. If such were the case, in an eternal sense it may be as if they had not been done at all. When these acts are performed by those with righteous motives, desires, and intent, then the necessary and expected results occur. To whatever degree we fall short in our desires or intent, the results will be frustrated.

As we progress to each stage, we cannot leave the earlier stages undone, for this will frustrate our progress. However, if we stall at the earlier stages, we are like those described in Matthew 23:23–24: "Woe unto you, scribes and Pharisees, hypocrites! for ye pay tithe of mint and anise and cummin, and have omitted the weightier matters of the law, judgment, mercy, and faith: these ought ye to have done, and not leave the other undone. Ye blind guides, which strain at a gnat, and swallow a camel."

These harsh words were written about those who act out deeds of righteousness but are in reality something else in their hearts. They are exactly those described by Jacob as "looking beyond the mark." One of the important results of allowing the power of the Atonement to penetrate our hearts is that it will help purge those improper tendencies, encourage us to resist evil, prompt us to obey all the commandments, and guide us to attend to the more important or weightier matters of the gospel. We are thus obliged, with the Lord's continual assistance and by his grace, to choose to obey all of his commands, and especially to concern ourselves with the "weightier matters" such as mercy toward others—again, to help others obtain the enabling power of the Atonement, which help is our participation in the work of his grace.

When we understand that the Lord looks upon our desires and our intent, we may have an increase of hope. Through the Atonement the things that we fail to do but earnestly want and try to do are counted as righteousness in our behalf. Without the Atonement this would not be possible, and we would be left falling short in every way and excluded from the Lord's presence forever.

As we move toward the conclusion of this book, we will talk about hope in Christ—what it is, how we may find it, and why it is important to do so.

PART 4

A Change of Perspective: The Security of His Grace Gives Hope

Let us now resume our imaginary journey. This time we are going to attend a high priests group meeting. The instructor is a substitute, and we'll look in on him before the meeting; then we will join him in class. Isn't it fun to have control over time and space? As authors, we don't claim to have any extra insight about how things work in the hereafter; but you never know, it could be this convenient. Just say it, and it happens!

Brother Mark Patterson has just been asked by the high priests group leader on Saturday afternoon to fill in the next day for the regular instructor, who has become ill. Accepting the assignment, he begins to experiment with the lesson, which is titled "Hope in Christ."

The following morning, after enjoying the first two hours of meetings, Brother Patterson slips into an empty classroom and has a quiet prayer. He feels that he needs all the help he can get, as he really wants to make a difference with what is to be presented to the brethren.

Minutes later, when all the class members are present, the time is turned over to him.

Arranging his materials in front of him, and taking a deep breath, Brother Patterson begins. "Good morning, brethren. Brother Norris called yesterday and asked if I might teach today's lesson, which is titled 'Hope in Christ.'

"Now, to begin with, I would like to ask the question, what is hope?"

Lee Jorgensen raises his hand and says, "I think it's a positive feeling we have about the Savior's atonement . . . about it having place in our own personal lives."

"Thanks, Lee," Brother Patterson replies. "As always, Lee, you're right on target. Let me suggest this comparison between faith and hope: If faith is an assurance that the celestial kingdom exists, then hope is the expectation that we will go there."

"I think," Bruce Babcock speaks out spontaneously, "that *hope* in the gospel sense is synonymous with *expectation* or *assurance . . .* not with *wish.*"

"I've never made that delineation," Brother Patterson replies honestly. "These are all excellent comments. I want to move us along now with a question. How many of you *hope* to go to the celestial kingdom?"

As might have been expected, all hands are raised.

"Good," Brother Patterson says. "Now, let me ask another question: How many of you *expect* to go to the celestial kingdom?"

Perhaps not surprisingly, not one hand is raised in response.

"I suggest, brethren, that the two words *hope* and *expect* are synonymous in a gospel sense."

A lively discussion then ensues, and using the seventh chapter of Moroni as a guide, several relevant points are made. Brother Patterson then explains that he has recently visited with one of the sisters in the ward, whose name is courteously omitted.

"We were talking about exaltation," he says, "and this sister expressed real doubt about the probability of ever achieving it. So I asked her how long it had been since she had been baptized. She indicated that she had joined the Church over two decades ago.

"I then asked this sister what would have happened to her if she had suddenly died of natural but tragic causes immediately following her baptism and confirmation. In other words, to which kingdom would she have gone? After a moment of consideration, she said, 'To the celestial kingdom, I suppose.' I then asked her to which kingdom she would go if she died today. She was uncertain but was pretty sure it wasn't the celestial kingdom.

"Now, you should know, brethren, that this is a person with a good heart and great desires to serve her Heavenly Father. Still, she was very uncertain and did not want to answer me. I then asked, 'Do you mean that after two decades of trying to serve Heavenly Father—working as hard as you can, as hard as you know how—you have fallen behind where you were when you joined the Church? This doesn't seem like a very good plan, and from all I know it is certainly not Heavenly Father's plan.'

"Well, as we concluded our discussion a peaceful feeling was there, and I think that she felt more assurance that she was in good standing with Heavenly Father. It is a curiosity, isn't it, that many don't seem to have a real hope in the Atonement.

"I believe," he continues, "that in the world the devil counterfeits the true principle of hope. For example, let's consider the practice of gambling, and more specifically the lottery, which is widely accepted and patronized in states throughout the country. This is an expression of *false* hope, where everyone pays so that one person can win. By contrast, in the gospel *true* hope in Jesus Christ comes because one person paid so that everyone can win and nothing is left to chance.

"Now," he presses, glancing down at his watch, "our time is short, so let me present two additional thoughts. Last evening I was reading the *Lectures on Faith*. This is, as most of you know, a series of lectures prepared under the direction of the Prophet Joseph for the School of the Prophets, in Kirtland. In lecture 6, paragraph 2, the Prophet taught, 'An actual knowledge to any person, that the course of life which he pursues is according to the will of God, is essentially necessary to enable him to have that confidence in God without which no person can obtain eternal life.'

"In other words, brethren, when we have a 'perfect brightness of hope,' we will have clarity of direction, as well as the confidence that was described by the Prophet Joseph. It is the only true lottery, if you will—which of course is not a lottery at all, but a guaranteed outcome to the faithful."

Brother Patterson then draws the class to a close by citing a statement by President Howard W. Hunter, as found in the October 1993 *Ensign:* " 'I promise you in the name of the Lord whose servant I am that God will always protect and care for his people. We will have our difficulties the way every generation and people have had difficulties. But with the gospel of Jesus Christ, you have every hope and promise and reassurance. The Lord has power over his saints and will always prepare places of peace, defense, and safety for his people. . . .

" 'This faith and hope of which I speak is not a Pollyanna-like approach to significant personal and public problems. I don't believe we can wake up in the morning and simply by drawing a big 'happy face' on the chalkboard believe that is going to take care of the world's difficulties. But if our faith and hope are anchored in Christ, in his teachings, commandments, and promises, then we are able to count on something truly remarkable, genuinely miraculous, which can part the Red Sea and lead modern Israel to a place 'where none shall come to hurt or make afraid.'[1]

"Now, brethren," Brother Patterson concludes, "I ask— just why have we had our discussion on hope? For the sake of time, let me answer my own question. One of the most significant discoveries that come from a study of the Atonement is that because of the Lord's grace, we do not have to do what I call 'the work of the gospel' alone, or even prior to receiving his grace. When we recognize that fact, the doctrine of hope opens up in new ways. It is an assurance in Christ that while we are plodding along here on earth, we can still know— with certainty, by the Spirit—that the course we are on will lead us directly home.

"In the name of Jesus Christ, amen."

_____NOTES

1. Howard W. Hunter, "An Anchor to the Souls of Men," *Ensign,* October 1993, pp. 72–73.

CHAPTER FOURTEEN

Continuous Refinement: Moving Forward Under the Umbrella of Christ's Grace

We would like to introduce you to a friend who shall remain anonymous. We helped her change her story only a little to protect her privacy. The central idea and events actually occurred as described in her account of what she regards as a wonderful event in her life. Let's allow her to tell the story:

"I have discovered that the Atonement *can* play a part in helping me become perfect in Christ. While it is clear to me that this is a long-term project, nevertheless it is not hopeless. I now understand clearly that the Atonement is not just for sinners. Christ did not just pay for our sins; rather, he provided a way for us to reconstruct ourselves—with His help—in the pattern that he set.

"An example of this is my own personal battle with excessive anger. I never knew I had a temper until I became a mother. Sometimes when I said this in public, people smiled knowingly, as if to say, 'She's exaggerating.' Someone once said that 'insanity is contagious; we get it from our children.' I say that an angry disposition is contagious, and that we seem to get that from them too.

"I love my father and have learned more good things from him than I can ever repay. Even so, when I found myself losing my temper with my children, I blamed him—simply because he lost his temper with me. I would get frustrated when I became very upset with my four children, simply because I knew this wasn't a proper response. Regardless, I would still find myself falling into some of the patterns of behavior I had experienced in the home of my youth.

"While my children were still quite young, I flew to Provo, Utah, and attended an Education Week program. One of the speakers taught a concept that affected me and my family positively for years afterward. He suggested that we can repent for the sins of our parents by correcting inappropriate behavior handed down through family relationships. Upon my return to our home in Florida, I immediately began to apply this concept in my relationships with my children.

"Sometime later I was talking with my uncle, my father's brother, about his father, my grandfather. When I asked him about our grandfather's temper, he told me that my grandfather might have been classified as abusive. I then inquired about my grandfather's father, and found that he was an alcoholic and that he probably beat his children.

"As I reflected on what he said, I became very resolute. *This has got to stop,* I thought. *This problem with temper has been passed down through at least four generations!* My determination was to try to stop the process in my generation.

"Not long after I made this commitment, I determined that I would never again spank my children. To this day, I have kept this promise. I am not saying that this should be a standard for others, but I realized that I only spanked my own children when I was angry—usually *very* angry—and that there was simply no justification for this response. It seemed to me that hitting another person in anger, especially a small person, simply taught *them* to hit, and to live with anger in their own life.

"I am sorry to say that the idea I learned during Education Week did not become a spiritual project. I didn't pray and ask for Heavenly Father's help, nor for his forgiveness. I just turned my face to the sun, so to speak, and went to work on the problem.

"Now, after some time, I am happy to report that my resolve not to spank has been successful. My determination not to lose my temper has also been productive. However, over the years I still found myself in moments of anger that I did not like and was honestly embarrassed about. Though I believe that if others had seen my progress they would have been impressed and encouraged me, I was not satisfied.

"One example of progress comes to mind. During a time when I was serving in the ward Primary presidency, I was sitting with my family in sacrament meeting. My husband, who was then serving as bishop, was on the stand, and I was 'managing the troops' by myself. Jeff, our four-year-old son, was sitting at the far end of the row, and began to act up. I tried to signal to him with some subtlety, but he, being a four-year-old, would have nothing of that. It was like he was mocking me and saying, 'We're in a public place in front of your friends. What are you going to do, yell at me right here in front of everybody?'

"I finally stood up, walked slowly down the row in front of our other children, and reached him. I took him gently by the arms—one of his in each of my hands—and lifted him up to me. I did not push my fingernails into his skin, although the thought occurred to me. I simply lifted him up gently and, knowing that others were watching, pulled him close in an apparent but deceptive show of 'mothering.' I then carried him into the foyer.

"Quickly I found a quiet and empty classroom. The idea came to mind that I would abandon my resolve about spanking and instead teach him a *real* lesson. But as I put him down on the floor and looked directly into his eyes, I realized that he was quivering. He was afraid of *me*, his mother!

"I then said to myself, *What have you done to this boy?* This sudden realization was overwhelming in its impact. I thought, *Oh dear, I am continuing the legacy of temper without knowing it. This has got to stop!* A wave of tenderness then came over me, and my heart softened.

"Remaining silent, I again looked into his eyes. I remembered the many feelings of love and joy I had experienced at the time of his birth. I remembered how much I enjoyed his mischievous personality and his fun-loving disposition. An eternity seemed to pass in a moment.

"Finally, I spoke his name softly. He responded, 'What, Mom?' I have to admit that he had not gone through any transformation; his words were unsteady and unsure.

" 'I love you, Jeffrey,' I replied.

" 'I love you too.' His voice seemed to express surprise and gratitude at my approach. He then just melted into my arms.

" 'Now, Jeff,' I whispered, 'do you think you can go back into the meeting and behave yourself?'

" 'Sure, Mom,' was his smiling response.

"I then lifted him gently to my side and carried him back into the meeting. Now he dutifully kept his promise—for about fifteen or twenty minutes! Still, the satisfaction I felt remained for a long time, even to this day—and now Jeff, serving a mission in Chile, is teaching Chilean children how to be reverent in their meetings.

"I have recently realized, however, that my struggle with anger had really been more of a self-help project than one of true repentance. I came to this conclusion while praying about my excessive temper, considering the power of the Atonement while doing so. In an instant, something changed deep inside of me. I felt the healing powers of the Atonement soothe and soften my disposition.

"The change inside me was immediate, yet gentle. A continuous reminder remains with me to this day. My Savior's enabling grace allowed me to change. However, I feel cautious within myself, and I try not to offend the tender Spirit that softened me, lest this Spirit be grieved and withdraw from me, leaving me to return to my old ways.

"In a recent Relief Society Spiritual Living lesson, the instructor unknowingly encouraged my progress as she quoted Elder Boyd K. Packer's counsel in a general conference address: 'To you adults who repeat the pattern of neglect and abuse you endured as little children, believing that you are entrapped in a cycle of behavior from which there is no escape, I say:

" 'It is contrary to the order of heaven for any soul to be locked into compulsive, immoral behavior with no way out! ...
" 'I gratefully acknowledge that transgressions, even those which affect little children, yield to sincere repentance. I testify with all my soul that the doctrine of repentance is true and has a miraculous, liberating effect upon behavior.' "[1]

As Elder Packer stated, the effects of the Atonement do not simply blot out transgression. Along with the payment for sin comes a wonderful transformation of the sinner. When the Lord intervenes and behavior changes, so does the heart of the penitent. This is true whenever we approach the Lord with a broken heart and a contrite spirit. Such knowledge truly gives us hope. With the Lord's help and by his grace we can become possessors of what Peter called "lively hope" (1 Peter 1:3), or a living assurance that we will one day return home to live eternally with those we love the most.

_____Notes

1. Boyd K. Packer, in Conference Report, October 1986, pp. 21–22.

CHAPTER FIFTEEN

"Lively Hope":
The Measured Effect of
Christ's Mercies

In July 1969, the United States placed the first man upon the moon. Apollo 11 filled us with wonder as we watched the landing of Neil Armstrong upon that foreign surface. In fact, more people around the world watched that event than any other incident in history.

But by April 1970, moon landing had become so commonplace that no one watched the takeoff of Apollo 13. In that moon landing mission, three men were on board what seemed to the outside world a routine mission to the earth's only natural satellite. Jim Lovell, Fred Haise, and Jack Swigert were in the midst of a great adventure. On the third day of the mission, with the lunar landing scheduled for the fourth day, a serious problem that came from a simple defect drew the world's attention, and millions watched while NASA turned its considerable resources to a new mission. No longer was their focus the moon landing; now it was a more critical issue. *Can we bring these men home safely?*

Gene Kranz was the NASA ground commander. As he directed the process, in mostly a calm and smooth manner, it seemed that one crisis after another rushed toward him. In the best of circumstances it is a delicate matter to bring a crew from space back to earth. Because the astronauts were flying in a damaged vehicle that had only limited power, the men on the ground created new uses for some of the equipment on board the ship in space.

Listening in on their conversations as portrayed in the movie *Apollo 13*, we hear a mixture of optimism and anxiety. Unmoved by any discouragement stood Kranz, the commander. When the president called to ask the odds of getting the astronauts back, Kranz challenged the others by saying, "We're not going to lose these men. Tell him we are not going to lose these men!"

Jim Lovell, the team leader aboard Apollo 13, was also supported by his mother, whose confidence didn't waiver. In an interview with the press, she told the nation, "If they could get a washing machine to fly, my Jimmy could land it."

At another moment, Kranz overheard his superiors saying, "This could be the greatest disaster in NASA history." His response was to correct them. "Not so, gentlemen," he stated. "This will be our finest hour!"

In encouraging his team, Kranz let them know that "failure was not an option. We're not going to lose them—not on my watch!"

The suspense continued to mount as the small spacecraft glided slowly toward earth. Minute, exact corrections of the angle of descent were performed with breathtaking concentration. If the craft approached on too shallow an angle, it would simply ricochet off the atmosphere, like a rock skipping across a pond, and be hurled off into space without hope of return. If the angle were too steep, the spacecraft could not withstand the heat—it would incinerate, and all inside would perish.

The possible damage to the craft's heat shield was unknown. If the shield had been seriously damaged, they could not withstand the heat, even if the angle of entrance was correct. All these and many other possibilities haunted the ground support crew while the spacecraft continued its seemingly slow but relentless journey home.

As the craft finally entered Earth's atmosphere, there was a moment when all contact was cut off between the craft and the control center in Houston. After that, their safe return would only be apparent by radio contact a few moments before they splashed into the sea. Adding to the drama, a typhoon warning was issued for the area at the edge of the landing zone.

As communication was cut off, it seemed that the whole world paused and everyone was holding their breath. A prominent newscaster said that "the whole world [was] watching." It seemed that never before had so many on the Earth been united in prayer. In the United States Congress, a resolution for a national prayer was passed. It was noted that the Pope led fifty thousand people in prayer in Rome. Thousands gathered at the Western Wall in Jerusalem, united in prayer. Another commentator said that the silence would last for three minutes. After that the fate of the crew would be apparent. If four minutes passed, it would be known that the outcome was tragic.

Three minutes passed, and no sound came across the radio. Four minutes passed . . . Tensions reached their peak as despair began to creep in. Then, as shown in the movie, almost magically the voice of Lovell crackled across the speaker. "Houston, this is Odyssey."

"Odyssey, Houston. Welcome home; we're so glad to see you." The room at ground control burst into applause, and the entire world joined in. The collective resources and faith of millions joined together to bring three men back to Earth—back home and back to their families.

As the two of us sat watching the motion picture of this remarkable event, we were touched with the similarity between the story portrayed on the screen and our earthly lives and missions. The Lord has said, "This is my work and my glory—to bring to pass the immortality and eternal life of man" (Moses 1:39). Is it reasonable to also suppose that we might hear, in response to a discouraging adversary, "This will be our greatest triumph! We'll bring them home!"

Can't you hear the Lord say, "We're not going to lose the faithful—not on my watch! We're going to bring them home!"

Are fewer resources utilized to bring us home than were used to bring home the Apollo 13 astronauts? Are fewer watching and waiting for our safe return? Will there be less joy when we successfully enter the heavenly atmosphere? The Lord has promised that we can return to him. Lively hope in Christ, then, includes an expectation that all preparations have been made, that there will be no surprises. If we continue on the path of righteousness, as outlined by the scriptures and modern prophets, that path will lead us safely home—and all this in the midst of the exultant joy of millions who have prayed for and sought our safe return.

CHAPTER SIXTEEN

Refining the Perspective: From Obscurity to Eternity

Over the past several years we have sincerely attempted to accept Elder Bruce R. McConkie's kindly solicitation to join him in the quest of "gaining a sound and sure knowledge of the Atonement."[1] We are certain that this journey will be a lifetime pursuit. As we paused for a moment and tried to consolidate our thoughts, we asked ourselves the following questions: What conclusions can we make now with some certainty? Can we refine our perspective after reading, reflecting, and responding?

From these strivings we developed a heightened awareness of three gospel truths. First, the atonement of Christ is the central event in all of human history, for which we have inexpressible gratitude.

Second, because of the Savior's grace we are not left alone, unaided in our quest to return home. Because he took upon himself our infirmities, his bowels are filled with mercy, and now he knows how to comfort and succor his children according to their infirmities. He not only *knows* how, but he *does* so continuously.

And third, in the midst of this life of struggle and turmoil, the truly penitent can find hope in Christ. This hope assures the faithful that the path upon which they walk actually leads to the celestial kingdom. They know that their exaltation is not yet assured, but they also understand that if they continue to press forward, they will ultimately arrive at the city of God and become citizens of that glorious community.

To illustrate these ideas, we want to describe a conversation between us as authors. To simplify, we have combined several discussions that took place over many months. The stories told are true but have been adjusted somewhat for the sake of privacy and propriety. The setting is the attic den of Brent's home, a comfortable room with a warm atmosphere, protected from the world by a grove of giant trees out the window to the south.

"Come in, Don." Brent speaks enthusiastically as his good friend walks into the entryway of his home. "Let's move right upstairs. I want you to tell me what's been going on since we talked last."

The two friends settle into a couple of the overstuffed chairs, prominent features of Brent's den. Brent turns down the stereo, which is playing Kenneth Cope's *My Servant Joseph* CD, and Don begins to review out loud the steps they have taken over the past several months to find answers to questions about grace and tender mercy. Don reminds Brent of their initial skepticism as they considered the possibility that they had not initially recognized some gentle and comforting doctrines of the kingdom. It had become apparent that somehow these truths had been there all along without their being aware of them. Don goes on to talk about their individual studies of the scriptures, their ongoing review of the writings of the modern-day prophets, and their careful reading of the works of other men of faith.

"So, Brent," Don begins slowly, "if you had to share a definition of grace right now, what would you say?"

"I think I would be cautious before I suggested a definitive once-and-for-all definition."

"I agree with you. Still, let me ask you to fill that out a little. Why are you cautious?"

"Oh, I suspect there are two or three reasons. One has to

do with the fact that the nature of the Atonement is infinite. How can a finite definition be given to the Lord's grace, which is a fundamental part of his infinite sacrifice?"

"That's a good question, Brent. Please continue."

"A second reason I have difficulty with a simple definition of grace is that even if we restrict the definition to a gospel context, the word *grace* is used to describe so many different actions."

"Give me some examples."

"Well," Brent says, his brow now furrowed, "there is the part of his grace that emanates or comes from Gethsemane— the sacrifice for the sins of the world. Then there is the part that is described in Alma chapter 7, saying that he will take upon him our sickness, our pains, and our infirmities. Additionally, there is the grace that is given to all because of the Resurrection. These elements of his grace are clearly unearned gifts, or even unearnable gifts."

"I can see what you're getting at. It surely is complicated, isn't it. Is there more to this?"

"Well, we can't leave out of our definition the grace expected of *us* as we serve others."

Kindly interrupting, Don adds, "I know what you are saying. We must include our part in the 'grace for grace' formula in any definition of grace."

"Exactly," Brent replies softly. "Let me make one further addition to our attempt to summarize the meaning of grace. A strict dictionary definition of grace states that grace is unconditional; yet we know that there *are* conditions to our receiving part of his grace. Do you see what I am getting at, Don?"

"Absolutely!" Don answers reassuringly. "I share the same thoughts. Now, let me recap for a moment. We can't come up with a short, once-and-for-all definition of grace because of its infinite qualities and the varied applications or uses of the word in the scriptures and the writings of the prophets. Is that what you're saying?"

"Yes, it is," Brent replies resolutely. "Let's extend our focus for a moment and consider an even broader explanation. Before we started studying this topic I believed that there was a simple formula: God had already done his part and now I have to do mine. Today I see less of a dividing line. I used to think of grace as 'the Atonement.' Now I see the Lord's grace—or *their* grace—as encompassing much of what Christ and the Father do for us. I used to feel more alone. Now, however, I feel that their grace plays a role in much of what I do each day, if I will let it happen."

"That's a major point, isn't it, Brent. By the Lord's grace, he is always there, ready to help. We always have our will, our agency, which is a gift from the Father and the Son—the right of moral choice. Because Christ and the Father will never violate our agency, some of the effects of their grace are less certain. When they offer the blessings of the gospel to us, we always have the right to choose to accept or reject their offer. If we accept, we then have the right to act upon our choice, which results in our taking responsibility for our actions. When we choose and respond righteously, Heavenly Father bathes us in the warm glow of his Spirit—encouraging us with the Savior's love and his grace. This grace plays a central role in our doing *our* part."

"Exactly!" Brent acknowledges enthusiastically. "Without making this the final, once-and-for-all statement about grace, these thoughts seem to express how I see or understand the meaning of grace today."

"Now, Don, it's my turn to ask *you* a question. In so doing, I should add that while it's good to have a working definition of grace, I think it's more important to determine how these changing definitions affect our lives. Thus, my question: After all this time of study, reflection or pondering, and trying to obey, what are your feelings as a result of gaining a new appreciation for his grace?"

"Well," Don smiles, "if I were to sum it up in a short sentence, I think I feel *acceptable*. I am beginning to be filled with hope. I don't mean this in a proud way, however, because by feeling acceptable, I don't necessarily mean *deserving*."

"Don, where do you think your feelings come from?"

"That's a good question," Don acknowledges, "because the answer is not as obvious as one might think. First of all, some of these growing feelings of hope originate from the

Spirit and seem to be deep inside of me. Also, and at least as important, is a temporal source of these feelings—the sort of 'here on the earth' source."

"Speak plain English, Don," Brent chides teasingly. "What do you mean?"

"Well, let me illustrate. During the five years we've been considering grace, the Church has been led by three different living prophets."

"I hadn't thought of that, but it is true. How does that apply here?"

"Well, along the way, as I studied the scriptures and the words of these great men, I would think about what I knew of them. I would also listen to their messages during each general conference. When considering their lives, reading their sermons, or listening to their words, I felt the tender entreaties of the Spirit encouraging me to be a better person. I listened to President Benson call for us to read the Book of Mormon and come unto Christ, and I really tried to follow his counsel.

"I also found great comfort in the words of President Hunter found right here on the back of the August 1994 *Ensign*." Pausing as he picks up the magazine, Don continues: " '[The Lord] will . . . stand by us forever to help us see the right path, find the right choice, respond to the true voice, and feel the influence of his undeniable Spirit. His gentle, peaceful, powerful persuasion to do right and find joy will be with us "so long as time shall last, or the earth shall stand, or there shall be one man upon the face thereof to be saved" ' (Moroni 7:36).

"Now, from these two prophets," Don concludes, "I felt that there was much to do, but that with the Lord's help it was possible. It seemed that they were saying that the Lord will not give up on me, in spite of my weaknesses."

"I see what you mean, Don. Can you think of any specific examples with our current prophet, President Hinckley?"

"I was just thinking about that. In 1995, President Hinckley came out to Massachusetts for a regional conference. He was accompanied by Elder Neal A. Maxwell. During the meeting Elder Maxwell gave a penetrating address on the Atonement. No one who truly listened could have heard his description of the love of the Savior, as manifested by his sacrifice, without weeping in gratitude—and, I might add, many of those in the congregation did so. Then, to add a wonderful dimension to that talk, President Hinckley followed with a powerful sermon. While speaking, the prophet simply encouraged us to be better people. It was made clear by his tone of voice as well as by his words how much he loves each of us personally—and by extension, then, how much the Lord loves and cares for us.

"Such experiences," Don says, "have made me feel acceptable—not finished, but *acceptable*. Again, I don't say this proudly; in fact, sometimes I am really overwhelmed by very personal feelings of unworthiness. Nevertheless, I feel that Heavenly Father loves and accepts me. I am certain that I have much to do along the path, but it seems that it is okay for us to feel that we are really on the road that will take us home. I'm not referring to you and me specifically, but to all members of the Church who have righteous motives, desires, and attitudes—those who, in spite of their weaknesses, are making a concerted effort to have a pure heart."

"When you use the words *motives, desires,* and *attitudes,*" Brent replies, "I am reminded of Elder Dallin H. Oaks's book *Pure in Heart,* wherein he teaches about the 'inner man' in ways I'd not previously considered."[2]

"That's where my connecting these three words comes from," Don rejoins. "Elder Oaks suggests that these three elements make up the inner man: our *desires,* or what we want to do with our time; our *motives,* or why we want to do what we want to do; and our *attitudes,* or our disposition, opinion, mental set, and so forth. As Elder Oaks delineated these elements of our inner selves, I really began to search my heart. I sense there is a tie-in between a person's inner self and grace. Such a connection has been one of our most important discoveries."

"It is sobering to consider, isn't it," Brent adds. "Now, Don, there are wonderful gifts of knowledge that come through studying, praying, and living. Is there more to it than that?"

"Since you've asked, Brent, I'll tell you what has recently taken place. Now, you know me very well, so it will probably not come as any surprise to you to know that in spite of my apparent self-confidence, I really have not felt that I could ever make it to the celestial kingdom. I look around at those who have given so much to the kingdom—men and women whose entire lives have been filled with selfless devotion. Their abilities and accomplishments so outstrip mine that I am left with a feeling that I'll simply never measure up. Do you know what I mean?"

"Of course," Brent responds honestly. "I've often felt that way myself."

"I'm glad to know that," Don replies. "Misery *does* love company."

They both laugh, and then Don asks, "Does all of this make sense?"

"I think," Brent replies, "that such a feeling of inadequacy is one of the occupational hazards of being part of a kingdom where perfection is the goal. It is also a sad result of living in a larger natural culture that stresses competition and winning. Somehow I think we're all seduced by the worldly quest to 'get ahead.' When I see so many in the Church who seem to be far ahead of me, it's easy for me to become discouraged."

"Frankly, Brent, it's comforting to hear you say that. It adds to my sense of reassurance that some of our conclusions about the Lord's tender mercies are valid."

"Let me reinforce what you just said," Brent enthuses. "Do you remember me talking about Merrill Wilkinson [a fictional name], my good friend and a stake president?"

"I think so," Don answers slowly.

"During the past several weeks," Brent continues, "he and I have talked a lot about hope and the Lord's tender mercies. In that context he shared some experiences he had with members of his stake—his parishioners, as he affectionately calls them.

"Apparently President Wilkinson was recently approached by a man and his wife who had raised a wonderful family and were truly striving to keep the commandments. The man never served in any prominent positions, and he and his family lived lives of relative obscurity. They were somewhat discouraged by their apparent lack of achievement and, as a couple, thought themselves unworthy to ever gain entrance into the celestial kingdom.

"The husband spoke frankly when he asked President Wilkinson, 'Can anyone like me really make it?'

"President Wilkinson then explained some important ideas by using his own experiences. Speaking directly to the husband, President Wilkinson said, 'Now, brother, I won't try to answer that for you personally, but let me share one or two experiences which seem to shed light on the possibilities. Many years ago I became acquainted with an educator, a high school shop teacher, and his wife. As time went on I learned that on one occasion this man had been sent by assignment to visit former members of the Church who had been sentenced to serve time in the state prison. After a few visits this man became concerned about the well-being of *all* the prisoners. This led to regular visits of support and caring.

"'At one time, while he was learning how to help others in this way, he came to me seeking a priesthood blessing. The words of the blessing were both astonishing and understandable. The message that I felt and tried to convey was that he could have the comfort of knowing that his life, to that point, was acceptable to the Lord. And if he continued on as he was going, he would ultimately find himself among the saints and angels of heaven.

"'Now,' President Wilkinson continued, 'let me share another example. Not long ago a young full-time missionary from out West was assigned to our stake. He was from a rural town somewhere in the western desert. He lacked many of the social graces common to others. His self-esteem was suffering, and he came to me seeking a blessing of comfort. As I laid my hands on his head, I was overwhelmed by the feeling of love that the Lord had for this common, obscure young missionary. When he came to me I only saw what I thought were his obvious earthly flaws and problems. The Spirit taught us both about his eternal future. He was told in the blessing that he will be welcomed home with outstretched arms by a Father who loves and cares for him.

" 'You know, my friends,' President Wilkinson reflected as he spoke to the couple in his office, 'not long ago I saw this same lad in a bookstore in Salt Lake City. I was out there visiting family. We embraced as he recounted the words of that blessing and told me how that experience opened up his life. He also introduced me to his new bride, whom he had recently married in the temple. He wanted me to know that he was still on the path, and was bringing others with him.

" 'Now,' President Wilkinson added, 'I'll share just one other. Not long ago I was asked to give a blessing to a member of our stake, a quiet woman of modest means. She recently had had a tracheotomy, the cutting of a permanent opening in her throat, which restricted her speech. Although she always covered her neck with a scarf, she could speak only with a raspy voice and was very hard to understand. She was self-conscious about her condition, and to say that only a few people avoided her would probably be too charitable.

" 'In a time of discouragement, this sister came to me seeking a blessing. I laid my hands on her head, wondering what I might say that would boost her spirits. I was immediately filled with the Spirit. I learned that Heavenly Father saw her in a different light than most others saw her. I told her that the celestial kingdom was within her grasp. Her place at the table in the kingdom of God was set, and he looked forward to her return. These words of comfort were almost electrifying for this sister, as well as for me, her stake president.

" 'I later learned that during the previous school year, this sister arose every morning before five o'clock, dressed, and drove throughout our expansive ward. She picked up several young people who otherwise would not have been able to make it to early-morning seminary. She did this without fanfare; in fact, few others knew about it.

" 'One who did know was a young Haitian boy from a broken home. Every morning this sister drove to his house, helping to provide him a way to learn of the Lord and his gospel.

" 'During that year, while studying under the tutelage of

a marvelous and dedicated teacher, this young Haitian experienced an awakening to spiritual values. His life changed. He obeys the commandments now with a new energy and is committed to going on a mission. Where would he be without the tender caring of an obscure woman who cannot adequately speak words of love—she can only live them? The Haitian boy now lives a significantly altered life because a caring servant set her alarm and quietly went about the Lord's work.'"

As the echoes of the stake president's stories gently subside, Brent concludes. "What's comforting about these stories, Don, is that I feel that they are about people like me. They give me great hope. I feel a little awkward in saying that since having the conversation with President Wilkinson, but I have had a gentle spiritual confirmation that Heavenly Father sees me in a similar way. I feel more acceptable to him now than ever before."

"How have those feelings affected your understanding of the doctrines of the Atonement and grace?" Don inquires.

"Maybe it isn't obvious," Brent replies, "but these things have had a profound effect on me. Don, I really am trying to do my best. With all that I am learning, I am beginning to accept the idea that by the Lord's grace, the combined effects of my trying to do my best and his providing of the Atonement will be enough to lead me home. This is *hope,* an assurance that if I keep going as I am, while making steady improvements with his help and encouragement, even someone like me can make it."

"I understand what you're saying, Brent," Don says. "It reminds me of a Sunday a while ago. I walked into stake priesthood meeting and sat down next to one of the men in our stake who is looked upon by many as a source of great spiritual insights. I have such respect for him that whenever he speaks I really try to pay attention.

"Anyway, as I slid into the pew where this brother was sitting, he pointed to a member of the ward who was sitting in a row just ahead of ours. He then quietly commented, '*There* is someone who is going to the celestial kingdom, and he doesn't even know it.'

"The person he singled out was an adviser to one of the Aaronic Priesthood quorums in the stake. As such, he had turned the lives of many boys toward missions and temple marriage. He had never held any other prominent position in the ward or stake. Nevertheless, I believe that the statement made about him was surely true; his life was a witness of his eternal condition."

"I know what you mean, Don," Brent sighs while shaking his head. "I was talking the other day to our good friend Ed Dennis, who now lives in the northwest. He indicated that while he was serving in a stake presidency, he conducted a temple recommend interview with a sister who lived a quiet life but who filled her time with kind acts of caring and support of the less fortunate. At the end of the interview, the counselor felt the Spirit testify of the love that Heavenly Father had for her. He sensed that not only was she worthy to enter the temple, but she was also worthy to return home and live eternally with God.

"After he completed the interview, and in an attempt to encourage this sister, Ed asked her where she thought she would go if she were to die that very night. She answered that she didn't know, but was pretty sure that it wouldn't be the celestial kingdom. Though she couldn't think of anything specific that would 'keep her out,' she just didn't see her life as being important enough to be there. Ed spent the next several minutes teaching her what the Spirit had testified to him—that she was worthy to have hope in Christ—the hope which is an assurance that the path she is on leads to the celestial kingdom.

"Anyway, Don, Ed told me that the woman left the interview filled with a new, though humble, confidence. And Ed left the meeting with the resolve to encourage all worthy members in a similar fashion—which he did thereafter."

"Brent," Don interjects, "as I think about all this, I can't help but remember an experience which, while a little embarrassing, also supports this notion. Almost twenty years ago I was called to serve as a counselor in a stake presidency. One of my very best friends lived in the stake. With our wives we had done some things socially, so I became acquainted with my friend's wife. She and I teased each other a lot. Over time the teasing kind of degenerated into little sarcastic jabs. I suppose, however, that if I could hear our barbs now, I'd be embarrassed. I should add," Don continues, looking for a little assurance, "that I was probably the cause of most of it, if you can believe that!"

"I can't imagine such behavior from you, Don," Brent smiles.

"Thanks. In any event, my sarcastic teasing seemed at the time to be harmless fun—although at someone else's expense. Anyway, not long after my call to the stake presidency, I was at the stake offices when this friend and his wife arrived for a temple recommend interview. When she saw the stake president, she said something like, 'I'm here for our recommend interview, and I don't want Don Mangum to do it. It just wouldn't feel right.'

"Now, this sister wasn't being critical, just honest. Given the nature of our relationship, she couldn't quite adjust to my new calling. Nonetheless, our stake president sent her to be interviewed by me.

"At first the interview was a little awkward for both of us. As we came to the formal part of the interview, however, there was an immediate change in the room. It is hard to describe what happened inside of me, but I gained a new appreciation for the meaning of the spirit of discernment.

"I can only say that the Holy Spirit taught me about the eternal identity of this woman. Expressions like 'royalty,' 'daughter of light,' and 'person of great worth' do not fully describe the insights that flooded into my mind. I gained somewhat of an understanding of the great love and respect and appreciation that Heavenly Father had for this particular daughter, who was at that moment in the room with me. I could feel the power of her worthiness. The feeling was so profound that I have never been able to tease her again. In fact, whenever I have see her, I am still filled with a sense of awe in remembering the message of that evening."

"That's a wonderful story, Don," Brent whispers genuinely.

"I think I learned two important lessons that night," Don continues. "The first concerned the real identity of my friend's wife. I came to know that she was an 'elect lady,' a queen, temporarily in a lesser state but of no less majesty.

"The second lesson came after several years of reflection. I think that we cannot truly understand how each person in the Lord's kingdom is valued by him. It would be folly to assume that the apparently 'average' members were not among the elect in the pre-earth life. This discovery has helped me treat more respectfully all those in the congregations I have attended."

"I've had similar impressions over the years," Brent adds. "While you were talking, I remembered a story a friend told me. He was serving as bishop at the time. When conducting his first series of tithing settlement interviews, he was astonished to find so much discouragement among the members of his ward. When he congratulated the many people who came and declared themselves full tithe payers, almost without exception they began to list the things that they were not doing well. There was no list of significant transgression, just a list of failure to do everything that was 'expected.'

"I think I have seen similar concerns in wards where I have lived," Brent continues. "But this bishop learned about the Lord's perspective regarding his children who desire to do what is right. My friend addressed this common malady of inappropriate discouragement by having a faithful counselor develop a theme of hope in a sacrament meeting. The counselor found a wonderful talk by Elder Neal A. Maxwell on the topic. Among other things, Elder Maxwell taught that we must learn to discern between 'divine discontent and the devil's dissonance.'³ The counselor taught that the Lord encourages and the devil discourages. He used more of Elder Maxwell's ideas to teach that we're much closer to the city of God than we think. These words of encouragement from one of the Lord's Apostles became an overriding theme for the time of service of that bishopric."

With these comments, Brent concludes his story. Shortly thereafter Don leaves Brent's home—each again enriched by the lively discussion, and looking forward to another.

In reality, conversations like these have in recent years usually been long-distance over the phone. As has no doubt been the case with most of you, friendships help make gospel living easier. Gospel discussions provide insights and motivation, while allowing meaningful friendships to deepen.

In the illustrations presented in this conversation, we had a simple objective. In all of these cases, and many others that might be shared, there is a common thread. In the midst of all of our efforts to become like Christ, it is possible to become impatient and create unrealistic expectations. Sometimes we think that the law of eternal progression is going to be repealed before we get it all together. The prophets, on the other hand, have been serious and consistent in their use of the phrase "eternal progression." Becoming too impatient can cause us to become discouraged. This condition may result in a loss of desire to even continue trying.

Our experience in studying the Atonement has confirmed a fundamental concept. Faithful Latter-day Saints are entitled to *hope*. It is "hope in Christ" that is the assurance that the path we are on leads to the celestial kingdom—and this because of Christ's atonement.

The feeling that we can't ever do enough is one of the causes of our losing confidence in our future and in losing hope. Two other causes come to mind. The first is expressed in a wonderful poem by an unknown author:

From Obscurity to Eternity

"Father, where shall I work today?"
My love flowed warm and free.
He pointed out a tiny spot, and said,
"Go there, tend that for me."

"Oh, no, not that!" I gasped,
"No one will ever see,
No matter how well my work is done.
Not that little spot for me!"

The answer he gave was not stern;
He spoke so tenderly,
"Little one, search that heart of thine.
Art thou working for them or me?

Nazareth was a little place,
And so was Galilee."

It is true that we can become unnecessarily discouraged when we think that what we are doing is not significant enough. Perhaps this little poem will help change that perspective.

Second, we can also develop a negative attitude when we compare our lot with others who seem to have more going for them. Elder Bruce R. McConkie taught us how to deal with this feeling of inadequacy in his book *The Promised Messiah*. Elder McConkie states: "Apostles and prophets do not gain precedence with the Lord unless they earn it by personal righteousness. The Lord loves people, not office holders. Every [member] is entitled to the same blessings and privileges offered the apostles. . . . All of the [members] in the kingdom are expected to live the law as strictly as do the members of the Council of the Twelve, and if they do so live, the same blessings will come to them that flow to apostles and prophets."[4]

It has been our hope, in this work, to present ideas and thoughts that will help make others see more clearly the benefits of the Atonement and how to access them. Perhaps it has all just been a reminder of things you have already known. Nevertheless, we have sought to reinforce the idea that when the power of the Atonement becomes internalized, it can mature until it is a personal part of our lives each day. This happens when, through the Lord's infinite grace, our experiences confirm our beliefs. At that point we can obtain the comforting hope that we are moving in the right direction.

As we press forward, we have the consolation of knowing that it is not all up to us. The Lord's amazing grace and his tender mercies will support us in this life, as they did before we got here. Thus, armed with that brightness of hope, we strive to become like him, consumed by the work of grace.

_____NOTES

1. Bruce R. McConkie, "The Purifying Power of Gethsemane," *Ensign,* May 1985, p. 10.
2. See Dallin H. Oaks, *Pure in Heart* (Salt Lake City: Bookcraft, 1988).
3. Neal A. Maxwell, *Deposition of a Disciple* (Salt Lake City: Deseret Book Co., 1976), p. 29.
4. Bruce R. McConkie, *The Promised Messiah* (Salt Lake City: Deseret Book Co., 1978), p. 594.

CONCLUSION
_____

The Nature
of Grace

This is an attempt on the part of the authors to organize a short list of the impressions and thoughts we have had regarding the doctrine of the Atonement and its implications and effects. We urge you to examine the endnotes, which include scriptural passages and remarks of prophets, Apostles, and faithful Saints that add depth and understanding. We have also shared other scriptural references that may provide the basis for further study.

1. Jesus Christ, the second member of the Godhead, condescended[1] to come to earth. In so doing, he volunteered[2] to do the will[3] of the Father and was chosen to fulfill the Father's plan[4] for each of us, our Father's children.

2. In his condescension, Christ was born of Mary and God the Eternal Father, making Christ the literal Son of God in the flesh[5]—which gave him unique powers and characteristics.[6]

3. In Gethsemane and on Calvary, Christ suffered for the transgressions of all mankind,[7] making repentance possible for all,[8] which repentance leads to exaltation for the truly penitent.[9]

4. After living a sinless life, during which he sought only his Father's will, Christ broke the bands of death for all the

Father's children through his resurrection.[10] Without the miraculous events outlined in items 1–4, we would have been left as spirits in endless misery to live forever with and in subjection to the devil and his hosts.[11]

5. While the effects of his atonement permeate all of creation,[12] when we individually come unto Christ with broken hearts and contrite spirits, we initiate the power of the Atonement in our personal lives.[13] The key or crucial turning point is for us to respond to the entreaties of the Spirit to soften and make our hearts malleable to the changes that will of necessity occur.[14]

6. As we come unto Christ with a broken heart and a contrite spirit, we find that it is through his grace and not our works that salvation or exaltation is made *possible*—though not *guaranteed*.[15] (With few exceptions, the words *salvation* and *exaltation* as used in the scriptures, are synonymous and are used interchangeably.[16])

7. Not only is the Atonement given by the Lord's grace, but it is his grace that enables us to gain salvation after all we can do.[17] Additionally, and most important, his grace also enables us to do all we can do.[18]

8. As Bruce C. Hafen has said, "The atonement is not just for sinners."[19] In addition to suffering for our sins to satisfy the demands of justice, Christ suffered our pains, our sicknesses, our disappointments, and our failures so that he could help us in our extremities.[20]

9. A significant key to understanding the power of the Atonement is this: As we move toward exaltation, we must progress from grace to grace, receiving grace for grace, in the pattern set by the Savior.[21]

10. To receive grace for grace suggests that while we engage our lives in the Lord's service by helping others come unto him, he is continuously giving us blessings beyond anything we merit by ourselves.[22] To progress from grace to grace includes our moving through levels of spiritual growth and development under the influence and effects of his favor and love.[23]

11. Gaining hope in Christ is an inherent effect of the Atonement upon those who come unto him.[24] This hope is an

assurance that the path we are on is leading us to exaltation.[25] True hope, like faith, embraces varying degrees of strength and constancy.[26] A "perfect brightness of hope" (2 Nephi 31:20) encompasses the expectation that we will obtain eternal life. Hope in Christ, as both a condition and a process, is a blessing to which all Saints are entitled and for which we should all diligently seek.[27]

12. Attaining exaltation requires a certain condition of the heart.[28] Good works are a necessary expression of the growth of that condition in each individual.[29] Additionally, performing these good works and becoming submissive to the Father are the means through which our hearts are transformed[30] as we become more and more like the Master.

13. Because of a lifetime of familiarity with the Atonement, we, the authors, have simply underestimated the power and effects which can come from this remarkable and miraculous blessing, this marvelous gift of God.[31]

14. In summary, the atonement of Christ is difficult to comprehend. It must be studied to be understood. Additionally, such understanding must be internalized by those who will gain the full advantage of the Atonement in this life and in the life to come. This essential study provides wonderful opportunities to understand and participate in the work of grace.

———Notes

1. 1 Nephi 11:16–33. In this remarkable vision Nephi is taught somewhat concerning the meaning of Christ's condescension. Note especially the verses that follow the angel's command in verse 26, "Look and behold the condescension of God!"

See also chapter 7 in this book.

2. As recorded in Abraham 3:27, Abraham's description of the pre-earth council in heaven is insightful: "And the Lord said: Whom shall I send? And one answered like unto the Son of Man: Here am I, send me. And another answered and said: Here am I, send me. And the Lord said: I will send the first."

3. Among numerous examples of the Lord's submission to the will of his Father, we find the Father's description in Moses 4:2: "But, behold, my Beloved Son, which was my Beloved and Chosen from the beginning, said unto me—Father, thy will be done, and the glory be thine forever."

The Savior's definition of the gospel is both instructive and profound as he taught the Nephites in 3 Nephi 27:13: "Behold I have given unto you my gospel, and this is the gospel which I have given unto you—that I came into the world to do the will of my Father, because my Father sent me." A more complete definition of the gospel follows in the next verses.

See John 6:38 as a New Testament example of Christ describing his mission as submission to the will of the Father. See also D&C 19:2, 24.

4. Moses 4:2, quoted above, is a clear example that the plan of salvation was the plan authored by the Father and fulfilled by the Son.

5. Nephi was taught the following by the angel: "And he said unto me: Behold, the virgin whom thou seest is the mother of the Son of God, after the manner of the flesh. And it came to pass that I beheld that she was carried away in the Spirit; and after she had been carried away in the Spirit for the space of a time the angel spake unto me, saying: Look! And I looked and beheld the virgin again, bearing a child in her arms." (1 Nephi 11:18–20.)

6. Christ himself taught us of his divine sonship and of his unique characteristics when he said in John 5:26: "For as the Father hath life in himself; so hath he given to the Son to have life in himself." See also John 10:17–18 and James E. Talmage, *Jesus the Christ* (Salt Lake City: Deseret Book Co., 1973), p. 22.

7. The prophet Lehi taught in 2 Nephi 2:9–10: "Wherefore, he is the firstfruits unto God, inasmuch as he shall make intercession for all the children of men; and they that believe in him shall be saved. And because of the intercession for all, all men come unto God; wherefore, they stand in the presence of him, to be judged of him according to the truth and holiness which is in him."

Jacob taught: "And he cometh into the world that he may save all men if they will hearken unto his voice; for behold, he suffereth the pains of all men, yea, the pains of every living creature, both men, women, and children, who belong to the family of Adam" (2 Nephi 9:21).

8. Second Nephi 26 is part of a several-chapter discussion by the prophet Nephi concerning the preeminent role and importance of the Messiah. In verses 26–28 he wrote:

Behold, hath he commanded any that they should depart out of the synagogues, or out of the houses of worship? Behold, I say unto you, Nay.

Hath he commanded any that they should not partake of his salvation? Behold I say unto you, Nay; but he hath given it free for all men; and he hath commanded his people that they should persuade all men to repentance.

Behold, hath the Lord commanded any that they should not partake of his goodness? Behold I say unto you, Nay; but all men are privileged the one like unto the other, and none are forbidden.

9. In Alma 42:24 the prophet Alma, himself an expert on penitence, taught his son Corianton of the necessity of sincere and heartfelt repentence: "For behold, justice exerciseth all his demands, and also mercy claimeth all which is her own; and thus, none but the truly penitent are saved."

See also Alma 26:21; 27:18.

10. In 1 Corinthians 15 the Apostle Paul presented his well-known discussion on the Resurrection. In verse 22 he taught us, "For as in Adam all die, even so in Christ shall all be made alive."

11. The Nephite prophet Jacob recorded these chilling words in 2 Nephi 9:8–9: "O the wisdom of God, his mercy and grace! For behold, if the flesh should rise no more our spirits must become subject to that angel who fell from before the presence of the Eternal God, and became the devil, to rise no more. And our spirits must have become like unto him, and we become devils, angels to a devil, to be shut out from the presence of our God, and to remain with the father of lies, in misery, like unto himself."

See also Alma 42:6–13.

12. To enumerate all the far-reaching effects of the Atonement is beyond both the scope of these statements and the ability of the authors. However, the prophets have long taught us of the undefinable nature of Christ's earthly mission. Again referring to the prophet Jacob, we find in 2 Nephi 9:7: "Wherefore, it must needs be an infinite atonement—save it should be an infinite atonement this corruption could not put on incorruption."

See also 2 Nephi 2:7 and 3 Nephi 12:19.

13. Lehi shared the following: "Behold, he offereth himself a sacrifice for sin, to answer the ends of the law, unto all those who have a broken heart and contrite spirit; and unto none else can the ends of the law be answered" (2 Nephi 2:7).

14. King Benjamin, in his familiar address, taught us the necessity of our becoming prepared to humbly accept the influence of

the Holy Spirit in the transformation process. We find in Mosiah 3:19: "For the natural man is an enemy to God, and has been from the fall of Adam, and will be, forever and ever, unless he yields to the enticings of the Holy Spirit, and putteth off the natural man and becometh a saint through the atonement of Christ the Lord, and becometh as a child, submissive, meek, humble, patient, full of love, willing to submit to all things which the Lord seeth fit to inflict upon him, even as a child doth submit to his father."

15. Our behavior must conform to the laws of the celestial kingdom if we are to spend eternity there. In a stirring address at Brigham Young University entitled "What Think Ye of Salvation by Grace?" Elder Bruce R. McConkie taught:

> Does salvation come by grace, by grace alone, by grace without works? It surely does, without any question, in all its parts, types, kinds, and degrees.
>
> We are saved by grace, without works; it is a gift of God. How else could it come?
>
> In his goodness and grace the great God ordained and established the plan of salvation. No works on our part were required.
>
> In his goodness and grace he created this earth and all that is on it, with man as the crowning creature of his creating—without which creation his spirit children could not obtain immortality and eternal life. No works on our part were required.
>
> In his goodness and grace he provided for the Fall of man, thus bringing mortality and death and a probationary estate into being— without all of which there would be no immortality and eternal life. And again no works on our part were required.
>
> In his goodness and grace—and this above all—he gave his Only Begotten Son to ransom man and all life from the temporal and spiritual death brought into the world by the Fall of Adam. . . .
>
> There is nothing any man could do to create himself. This was the work of the Lord God.
>
> Nor did we have any part in the Fall of man, without which there could be no salvation. The Lord provided the way, and Adam and Eve put the system into operation.
>
> And finally, there neither has been, nor is, nor ever can be any way nor means by which man alone can, by any power he possesses, redeem himself. (In *Brigham Young University 1983–84 Fireside and Devotional Speeches* [Provo, Utah: University Press, 1984], p. 47.)

If this talk is carefully read—and we commend it to all—it is clear that Elder McConkie wanted us to understand the fundamental relationship between grace and performance. Both are necessary, even essential, but the Atonement, given to us by the Lord's grace, is the indispensable ingredient in order for our efforts to have any meaning whatsoever.

Further, the prophet Jacob explained in 2 Nephi 2:6–8 that:

> Wherefore, redemption cometh in and through the Holy Messiah; for he is full of grace and truth.
>
> Behold, he offereth himself a sacrifice for sin, to answer the ends of the law, unto all those who have a broken heart and a contrite spirit; and unto none else can the ends of the law be answered.
>
> Wherefore, how great the importance to make these things known unto the inhabitants of the earth, that they may know that there is no flesh that can dwell in the presence of God, save it be through the merits, and mercy, and grace of the Holy Messiah.

16. "Salvation in its true and full meaning is synonymous with exaltation or eternal life and consists in gaining an inheritance in the highest of the three heavens within the celestial kingdom. With few exceptions this is the salvation of which the scriptures speak." (Bruce R. McConkie, *Mormon Doctrine* [Salt Lake City: Bookcraft, 1966], p. 670.)

17. "This grace is an enabling power that allows men and women to lay hold on eternal life and exaltation after they have expended their own best efforts" (LDS Bible Dictionary, s.v. "grace").

18. The prophet Jacob gave us this important insight, found in Jacob 4:6–7: "Wherefore, we search the prophets, and we have many revelations and the spirit of prophecy; and having all these witnesses we obtain a hope, and our faith becometh unshaken, insomuch that we truly can command in the name of Jesus and the very trees obey us, or the mountains, or the waves of the sea. Nevertheless, the Lord God showeth us our weakness that we may know that it is by his grace, and his great condescensions unto the children of men, that we have power to do these things."

Further, the Bible Dictionary adds this important insight: "It is . . . through the grace of the Lord that individuals, through faith in the atonement of Jesus Christ and repentance of their sins, receive strength and assistance to do good works that they otherwise would not be able to maintain if left to their own means" (s.v. "grace").

19. In Bruce R. Hafen's book *The Broken Heart* (Salt Lake City: Deseret Book Co., 1989), the introduction is titled "The Atonement Is Not Just For Sinners." In this simple and provocative sentence is captured a dimension of the Master's sacrifice which we had pre-

viously never considered. Brother Hafen's discussion in that introductory chapter has added clarity and insight as we have attempted to expand our appreciation for the multiplicity of gifts which come from the atonement of the Savior. We encourage all to read the chapter and the book.

20. In Alma 7:11–12 the prophet Alma heightens our awareness of the deep compassion the Savior feels for each of us and why we may completely trust his capacity to understand and help us: "And he shall go forth, suffering pains and afflictions and temptations of every kind; and this that the word might be fulfilled which saith he will take upon him the pains and the sicknesses of his people. And he will take upon him death, that he may loose the bands of death which bind his people; and he will take upon him their infirmities, that his bowels may be filled with mercy, according to the flesh, that he may know according to the flesh how to succor his people according to their infirmities."

21. Doctrine and Covenants 93 contains many helpful passages that teach us about receiving "grace for grace" and moving from "grace to grace." Consider the following: "And I, John, saw that he received not of the fulness at the first, but received grace for grace; and he received not of the fulness at first, but continued from grace to grace, until he received a fulness" (verses 12–13). Further, in this same section we are taught concerning the process required of each of us. Consider: "I give unto you these sayings that you may understand and know how to worship, and know what you worship, that you may come unto the Father in my name, and in due time receive of his fulness. For if you keep my commandments you shall receive of his fulness, and be glorified in me as I am in the Father; therefore, I say unto you, you shall receive grace for grace." (Verses 19–20.)

22. Robert Millet, in his insightful book *By Grace Are We Saved*, wrote, "With divine assistance people are in a position to receive additional attributes and powers of the Spirit through repentance and subsequent faithfulness: they may receive what the scriptures speak of as 'grace for grace.' . . . To receive 'grace for grace' is to receive of the Father as we give to others." (*By Grace Are We Saved* [Salt Lake City: Bookcraft, 1989], p. 39.)

23. In teaching us of the process of moving from "grace to grace," the Prophet Joseph Smith indicated that becoming Godlike comes "by going from one small degree to another, and from a small capacity to a great one; from grace to grace, from exaltation to exaltation, until you attain to the resurrection of the dead, and are

able to dwell in everlasting burnings, and to sit in glory, as do those who sit enthroned in everlasting power" (*Teachings of the Prophet Joseph Smith,* comp. Joseph Fielding Smith [Salt Lake City: Deseret Book Co., 1976], pp. 346–47).

24. The prophet Mormon wrote to his son Moroni concerning hope, as recorded in Moroni 8:26: "And the remission of sins bringeth meekness, and lowliness of heart; and because of meekness and lowliness of heart cometh the visitation of the Holy Ghost, which Comforter filleth with hope and perfect love, which love endureth by diligence unto prayer, until the end shall come, when all the saints shall dwell with God."

25. Mormon adds some insight to this in Moroni 7:41: "And what is it that ye shall hope for? Behold I say unto you that ye shall have hope through the atonement of Christ and the power of his resurrection, to be raised unto life eternal, and this because of your faith in him according to the promise."

Elder Bruce R. McConkie wrote: "As used in the revelations, hope is the desire of faithful people to gain eternal salvation in the kingdom of God hereafter. It is not a flimsy, ethereal desire, one without assurance that the desired consummation will be received, but a desire coupled with full expectation of receiving the coveted reward." (*Mormon Doctrine,* p. 365.)

26. Elder McConkie wrote further concerning hope: "Faith and hope are inseparable. Hope enables men to have faith in the first instance and then because of faith that hope increases until salvation is attained." (Ibid., p. 366.) See also Moroni chapter 7, especially verses 40–44.

27. The prophet Moroni considered the necessity of hope in the lives of the Saints in Ether 12:32: "Wherefore man must hope, or he cannot receive an inheritance in the place which thou has prepared."

28. In 3 Nephi 9:20 the Lord taught the Nephites upon his arrival on this continent: "And ye shall offer for a sacrifice unto me a broken heart and a contrite spirit. And whoso cometh unto me with a broken heart and a contrite spirit, him will I baptize with fire and the Holy Ghost."

Further, the prophet Alma said to his wayward son Corianton in Alma 42:24: "For behold, justice exerciseth all his demands, and also mercy claimeth all which is her own; and thus, none but the truly penitent are saved." See also D&C 137:5–9.

29. It is difficult to express this thought in a single verse reference or short quote from a contemporary source. We do, however,

make reference to King Benjamin's address, especially the passages in Mosiah 4. In this chapter he reminds us of the close relationship between our labors and the Lord's tender influence upon us. We also suggest a reading of the thoughts contained in pages 7–9 of Bruce Hafen's *The Broken Heart.*

30. In Mosiah 3 King Benjamin taught about the transformation necessary in all of us, saying: "For the natural man is an enemy to God, and has been from the fall of Adam, and will be, forever and ever, unless he yields to the enticings of the Holy Spirit, and putteth off the natural man and becometh a saint through the atonement of Christ the Lord, and becometh as a child, submissive, meek, humble, patient, full of love, willing to submit to all things which the Lord seeth fit to inflict upon him, even as a child doth submit to his father" (verse 19).

31. We refer to Elder McConkie's remarkable conference sermon wherein he taught us all:

> Now, the atonement of Christ is the most basic and fundamental doctrine of the gospel, and it is the least understood of all our revealed truths.
>
> Many of us have a superficial knowledge and rely upon the Lord and his goodness to see us through the trials and perils of life.
>
> But if we are to have faith like Enoch and Elijah we must believe what they believed, know what they knew, and live as they lived.
>
> May I invite you to join with me in gaining a sure knowledge of the Atonement.
>
> We must cast aside the philosophies of men and the wisdom of the wise and hearken to that Spirit which is given to us to guide us into all truth.
>
> We must search the scriptures, accepting them as the mind and will and voice of the Lord and the very power of God unto salvation. ("The Purifying Power of Gethsemane," *Ensign,* May 1985, p. 10.)

As authors we have sought to set these thoughts of Elder McConkie to memory. Once there, we consider frequently the challenge set forth by this special witness of the Master. We know that we have not yet achieved the goal outlined here, we have yet far to go. But we have progressed a bit of the way and are grateful for the stirring motivation given by Elder McConkie and the spirit of the Lord.

Index

175